SHOP
BY MAIL
WORLDWIDE

SHOP
BY MAIL
WORLDWIDE

How to Find It, Buy It and Get It for Less—from China and Perfumes to Fashions and Toys

ANNE FLATO and
MARILYN SCHIFF

Illustrations by Elizabeth Whalen

Vintage Books
A Division of Random House
New York

A VINTAGE ORIGINAL, February 1987

Library of Congress Cataloging in Publication Data

Flato, Anne.
  Shop by mail worldwide.

Includes index.
    1. Mail-order business—Handbooks, manuals, etc.
2. Mail-order business—Directories. 3. Catalogs,
Commercial—Directories. I. Schiff, Marilyn,
1939–   . II. Title.
HF5466.F58   1987   380.1′029′4   86-40159
ISBN 0-394-74667-8

Manufactured in the United States of America

Acknowledgments

Our thanks to our husbands and children who helped out and pitched in while we were busy with the book; especially Jud, who was our computer maven.

We also wish to thank our friends, John and Sue in England, Sylvain and Celyna in France, Gerlinde in Germany and Harry in Austria, who helped locate some of our sources.

A special thanks to Judy, who helped put us in touch with the right people at the right time, and last but not least, our postman, who surely must have wondered about all the foreign mail he was delivering.

Contents

SHOP
BY MAIL
WORLDWIDE

Introduction

How It All Began

Approximately seventeen years ago we both moved into our new homes, one block apart, and renewed our old college friendship. Soon after, we each bought furniture for our dining rooms, but we didn't have much left in our respective budgets for the china and crystal that we desired.

Not willing to settle for less than Royal Doulton china, service for twelve plus soup, dessert and serving dishes, which at $34.00 a five-piece place setting was a great deal of money in 1970, we decided to write a letter to a store in England and find out whether we could order what we wanted directly.

The first store to which we wrote—bingo!—we got a price of about $300.00 for all the pieces we wanted, with mailing and insurance included. This was a saving of $300.00—enough for the crystal we wanted. Nothing but Waterford and Orrefors crystal for us! At the time Waterford was $14.00 a glass and Orrefors was $6.00. Of course we quickly found an Irish store willing to send Waterford at $7.00 a glass and a Danish store, which sent thirty-six pieces of Orrefors crystal for $75.00, including mailing and insurance.

Every piece arrived in perfect condition, so we were launched into a new mode of shopping.

After shopping around at home, whenever we wanted something that was manufactured in another country, we were usually able to find a store abroad willing to send it to us for 50 percent or less of the U.S. price. Thereafter we sent for Irish table linens, Waterford gift items, Rya rugs and many other items.

Many years have passed and now we are each in the remodeling and redecorating phase and we have added French porcelain, Chinese carpets and custom-made furniture to our homes. We have sent for wedding gifts and baby gifts, birthday and anniversary presents, and lately, replacements for dishes and crystal that have broken over the years.

When we realized how often we were shopping by mail around the world and how many catalogs we had collected, we decided it was time to write a book.

The value of the U.S. dollar makes shopping abroad very attractive. At some times it is more attractive than at others due to currency fluctuations, but shopping abroad is always a good value. However, not everyone has the time, money or inclination for such a trip. With this book you need not travel abroad to shop abroad. We will tell you not only where to find what you want, but how to go about getting it from there to here.

A note about currency conversions and price comparisons that you will see in the book: When a source quoted us a price in U.S. dollars we gave that price in the text, and if a price in foreign currency was included, we gave that as well. When we received the price in a foreign currency, we converted it at the time we received it. We put the converted number in parentheses. Therefore, if one company quoted us a price in May and another company quoted us the same price, in the same currency, in October, the dollar equivalents may be different due to the rate of exchange at the time we received the response.

The book is organized by type of merchandise and we have a separate category for department stores and general catalogs where you can write to find almost anything from anywhere. We have tried to make this a complete step-by-step guide to shopping abroad from your armchair.

We have alphabetized the stores within each chapter by the first letters of their names. It does not matter whether the first letter is an initial, a last name or a title. The only word that we did not alphabetize is the English word "the" when it came at the beginning of the store name.

We have indexed the shops by country, and given street as well as mailing addresses so that you can use this book when you do travel as well.

We gathered the source material for this book by writing letters to shops we have visited during our travels or have heard about from our friends and associates who live in or do business in foreign countries, and from ads in foreign magazines, hotel brochures, et cetera.

We did exactly the same thing that we are telling you to do. We wrote letters asking about specific items of interest and whether or not the store had a general catalog that it could send to us. Sometimes when we have listed only one or two brands of merchandise it is because the shop sent a response that was as specific as our inquiry. We then used "etc." or "and others" to indicate that you could write for other brands or items.

All of the sources listed responded to our letters, showed a willingness to deal by mail and offered worthwhile savings. No one paid to be listed in this book and we did not solicit any advertisements. In fact, none of the merchants knew we were writing a book when we asked for information.

How to Start

First you must do your homework: You must know what you want and what it costs locally. This will enable you to write a specific inquiry that will bring a response that contains all the information you need in order to determine the complete mail-order cost.

Here are some of the things that you may have to determine in advance, depending upon what type of item you are interested in: brand name, style and size, pattern name, quality, line density and/or stitches per inch, hand cut or machine cut, et cetera. You can clip ads from newspapers, magazines and brochures and whenever possible you should visit stores to see the item. Find out if the item is currently available or if your local store has to place a special order.

Plan ahead. Do you have the time to wait for the item if you send for it, or do you need it immediately? It's too late for next week's hostess gift but not too late to order a baby or wedding gift needed a few weeks or months in the future. Sometimes you can phone in an order to speed the ordering process.

If you can't find a specific listing for what you want, write to one of the department stores located in the country that makes the particular product.

Writing the Letter

When you write your letter, the simpler it is the better. Remember, English may not be the store-keeper's first language.

After you have decided what you want to purchase, browse through the listings in the chapters that follow and select the appropriate stores. It is best to type or clearly hand print your letter. Be specific in describing what you want. List the brand name, pattern name or number, size, quantity and color. If possible include a picture or photo of the item.

You should also ask for the cost of mailing and insurance and the total price in U.S. dollars. It is also a good idea to ask if the item is in stock for immediate delivery. Be aware that restocking of a particular item may cause a substantial delay in mailing time. (By waiting a month we saved $54.00 on a Waterford dish we ordered.)

Here is a sample letter to give you an idea of how easy it is:

Your street address
City, State, Zip code
U.S.A.
Date

Chinacraft of London
130 Barlby Road
London, England W10 6BW

Dear Sir:

I am interested in purchasing eight, five-piece place settings of the "Wild Strawberry" pattern by Wedgwood.

Each place setting is to consist of a dinner plate, salad plate, bread and butter plate and a cup and saucer.

I would also like a price for the large oval serving platter and the covered vegetable dish.

Please send me the complete price, including mailing and insurance, in U.S. dollars. Please indicate if you have deducted the VAT.

Are these items available for immediate delivery?

If you have a brochure listing all the pieces available in this pattern I would appreciate receiving one.

Thank you very much.

Sincerely,

Your Name

At this time airmail postage rates for letters are as follows:

Aerogramme	– $.36
½ oz.	– $.44
1 oz.	– $.88

Letters to Canada and Mexico take the same postage as local mail. An aerogramme, which costs only $.36, is a lightweight stationery item sold at the post office. This is the least expensive way to write to any other part of the world, provided that you are not enclosing anything.

For those of you who are in a hurry, or who have already written a first letter and are now ready to order, calling overseas is a relatively simple matter, and not as expensive as you might think. As always, dialing the call yourself is less expensive than getting operator assistance. You must also allow for the time differences around the world so that you don't call before the stores open or just as they are closing.

To call on AT&T:

1. Dial the international access code—011.
2. Dial the country code of the desired country.
3. Dial the city code.
4. Dial the local phone number. (NOTE: Not all numbers are seven digits.)

When we have given a phone number, we have given all four of the above. For further dialing information you can call the toll-free International Information Service number: 1-800-874-4000.

A further word on calling: Remember, unless you are calling an English-speaking country, or one with a special 800 number to facilitate phone orders, you may find yourself talking to someone who doesn't speak English. Companies may have staff people to answer English mail but they may not be available to answer your phone call.

Sizes

Gertrude Stein may have said, "A rose, is a rose, is a rose," but unfortunately a size, is not a size, is not a size, as we all know from experience with different styles and manufacturers right here at home. Sizes vary abroad as widely as they do here. Sizes are given in inches (32″–42″), in metric (38–50), and in the general Small, Medium, Large and Extra Large (S, M, L, XL). Casual bulky-style sweaters are usually S, M, L and XL, but if you're not sure that their M and your M are the same, send the measurements of a similar type sweater that you have that fits you well. Make a diagram such as this

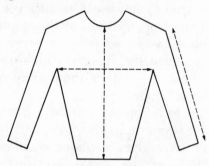

and measure the width across the chest, the sleeve length and the length from neck back to the bottom. This is what we did when we ordered sweaters. Many companies include a diagram such as this in the brochure and suggest that they will choose the size that best fits your measurements.

English and American dress sizes are about one size apart. An American 10 is approximately equal to an English 12; a 12 is a 14, et cetera. Sweater sizes are about the same and given in inches: 32", 34", et cetera.

An American size S in a man's sweater is a British 34; an M is a 36/38; L is a 40; and XL is a 42/44.

On the Continent things get more complicated; here a man's size S is a 44; an M is a 46/48; an L is a 50; and an XL is a 52/54.

When our friend Sue from Great Britain was visiting, she forgot her sneakers. She said she had a large foot and wore a 6½. She was able to borrow our size 8 tennis sneakers, but they were a tight fit. If you're embarrassed by your American women's size 9 shoes, the solution is to shop in Britain where you'll wear a modest 7½. Of course your size 9 will seem small compared to the equivalent French size, a 41. (A U.S. 7 is a 5½ in Britain and a 38 in France.) We also did some shopping when we were in Spain, where our size 8½ feet fit into lovely size 39 leather pumps. Remember that both foot shape and size influence the fit. You will be most successful if you wear a European shoe and you order the same brand. Then you can order the size and styles that you know are comfortable.

Men's shoe sizes also vary; a U.S. 9 is a British 7½, and a French 42½; a U.S. 10 is a British 8½, and a French 44. Once again, order a brand and size that you know to be comfortable.

For your convenience, the following are some conversions that may make ordering or selecting a size easier when metric measurements are used.

Centimeters (cm)	to	Inches		
1 cm	to	0.4	inches	
2.5 cm	to	1	inch	
1 meter to 100 cm	to	40	inches	
28.4 grams	to	1	ounce	
454.4 grams	to	1	pound	
½ kilogram	to	1.1	pound to	17.5 ounces
1 kilogram	to	2.2	pounds to	35 ounces

For liquid measurements, see the chapter on perfumes.

Other Currencies

Sometimes you will get a response and the price will not be given in dollars, or the brochure you asked for will give additional prices in the local currency.

A foreign exchange table can be found each day in the *Wall Street Journal*, usually available at your local library. You can also check the business pages of your local newspaper or call your local commercial bank.

Here is a sample Foreign Exchange Rate column.

FOREIGN EXCHANGE

The New York foreign exchange selling rates below apply to trading among banks in amounts of $1 million and more, as quoted at 3 p.m. Eastern time by Bankers Trust Co. Retail transactions provide fewer units of foreign currency per dollar.

Country	U.S. $ equiv.		Currency per U.S. $	
	Thurs.	Wed.	Thurs.	Wed.
Argentina (Austral) ...	1.2484	1.2484	.801	.801
Australia (Dollar)	.7200	.7105	1.3889	1.4075
Austria (Schilling)	.05368	.05325	18.63	18.78
Belgium (Franc)				
Commercial rate	.01854	.01833	53.95	54.55
Financial rate	.01834	.01820	54.52	54.95
Brazil (Cruzeiro)	.0001326	.0001326	7540.00	7540.00
Britain (Pound)	1.4280	1.4440	.7003	.6925
30-Day Forward	1.4233	1.4396	.7026	.6946
90-Day Forward	1.4159	1.4325	.7063	.6981
180-Day Forward	1.4080	1.4245	.7102	.7020
Canada (Dollar)	.7364	.7359	1.3580	1.3588
30-Day Forward	.7361	.7357	1.3586	1.3593
90-Day Forward	.7351	.7348	1.3604	1.3610
180-Day Forward	.7334	.7331	1.3637	1.3641
Chile (Official rate)	.005612	.005612	178.20	178.20
China (Yuan)	.3378	.3378	2.9607	2.9607
Colombia (Peso)	.006309	.006309	158.50	158.50
Denmark (Krone)	.1034	.1018	9.6700	9.8250
Ecuador (Sucre)				
Official rate	.01489	.01489	67.175	67.175
Floating rate	.009153	.009153	109.25	109.25

	U.S. $ equiv.		Currency per U.S. $	
	Thurs.	Wed.	Thurs.	Wed.
Finland (Markka)	.1751	.1739	5.7100	5.7490
France (Franc)	.1227	.1224	8.1500	8.1700
30-Day Forward	.1225	.1222	8.1640	8.1830
90-Day Forward	.1219	.1216	8.2025	8.2250
180-Day Forward	.1210	.1204	8.2650	8.3050
Greece (Drachma)	.007722	.007616	129.50	131.30
Hong Kong (Dollar) ..	.1285	.1285	7.7800	7.7800
India (Rupee)	.08562	.08432	11.68	11.86
Indonesia (Rupiah) ...	.0008897	.0008897	1124.00	1124.00
Ireland (Punt)	1.1635	1.1530	.8595	.8673
Israel (Shekel)	.0006734	.0006734	1485.00	1485.00
Italy (Lira)	.0005562	.0005488	1798.00	1822.00
Japan (Yen)	.004520	.004411	221.25	226.70
30-Day Forward	.004525	.004416	221.01	226.43
90-Day Forward	.004537	.004429	220.40	225.78
180-Day Forward	.004558	.004451	219.40	224.67
Jordan (Dinar)	2.6226	2.6226	.3813	.3813
Kuwait (Dinar)	3.2712	3.2712	.3057	.3057
Lebanon (Pound)	.05236	.05236	19.10	19.10
Malaysia (Ringgit)	.4111	.4072	2.4325	2.4555
Malta (Lira)	2.1793	2.1793	.4589	.4589
Mexico (Peso)				
Floating rate	.002717	.002632	368.00	380.00
Netherlands (Guilder)	.3328	.3317	3.0050	3.0150
New Zealand (Dollar)	.5430	.5350	1.8416	1.8692
Norway (Krone)	.1264	.1244	7.9100	8.0400
Pakistan (Rupee)	.06349	.06317	15.75	15.83
Peru (Sol)	.00007172	.00007172	13943.00	13943.00
Philippines (Peso)	.05370	.05370	18.62	18.62
Portugal (Escudo)	.006024	.006116	166.00	163.50
Saudi Arabia (Riyal) .	.2740	.2740	3.6500	3.6500
Singapore (Dollar)	.4678	.4640	2.1375	2.1550
South Africa (Rand) ..	.3970	.3970	2.519	2.5189
South Korea (Won) ..	.001121	.001121	891.90	891.90
Spain (Peseta)	.006188	.006184	161.60	161.70
Sweden (Krona)	.1251	.1234	7.9950	8.1050
Switzerland (Franc) ..	.4596	.4552	2.1760	2.1970
30-Day Forward	.4609	.4566	2.1696	2.1900
90-Day Forward	.4636	.4593	2.1570	2.1770
180-Day Forward	.4671	.4632	2.1410	2.1590

	U.S. $ equiv.		Currency per U.S. $	
	Thurs.	Wed.	Thurs.	Wed.
Taiwan (Dollar)	.02478	.02478	40.36	40.36
Thailand (Baht)	.03672	.03672	27.23	27.23
United Arab (Dirham)	.2723	.2723	3.673	3.673
Uruguay (New Peso)				
Financial	.009744	.009744	102.63	102.63
Venezuela (Bolivar)				
Official rate	.1333	.1333	7.50	7.50
Floating rate	.06944	.06944	14.40	14.40
W. Germany (Mark) ..	.3733	.3736	2.6790	2.6770
30-Day Forward	.3744	.3747	2.6710	2.6688
90-Day Forward	.3767	.3770	2.6549	2.6525
180-Day Forward	.3796	.3801	2.6342	2.6308
SDR	1.06081	1.04783	0.942676	0.954352
ECU	0.835293	0.819187	....	....

Special Drawing Rights are based on exchange rates for the U.S., West German, British, French and Japanese currencies. Source: International Monetary Fund.

ECU is based on a basket of community currencies. Source: European Community Commission.

z-Not quoted.

Find the country you need. If you use the U.S. dollars equivalent column, the number given indicates the value of one unit of foreign currency in U.S. dollars. For instance: If the listing for France says .1227, this means that the franc is worth just over 12¼ cents. Multiply .1227 by the number of francs that the item costs to get your price in dollars.

If you look at the currency per U.S. dollars column, and the number is 8.1500, this means that there are slightly more than 8 francs to the dollar. Here you have to divide 8.15 into the price given in francs to determine the cost in dollars.

Foreign exchange rates change daily, so be sure to

use a current newspaper to approximate your price. The price is only an approximation because there is sometimes a small bank charge for the deposit of a foreign check.

Most stores will accept your personal check and many will also accept American credit cards such as Visa, MasterCard or American Express. Do not send cash! When shops ask for bank drafts or checks in a foreign currency, you can get them at your local bank.

PLEASE NOTE: When responses are given in foreign currencies, a comma is often used where we use a period. For example: For 14 milliliters of perfume priced at 458,00 French francs, read 458 French francs. When you are quoted a price in U.S. dollars you must respond in a reasonable period of time as currency fluctuates and prices change.

Import Duty

The U.S. Postal Service sends all incoming foreign mail shipments to customs for examination. Those packages on which duty is due are given a mail-entry form showing duty owed. Your mail person will collect the duty owed plus a postal-handling fee of $2.50 upon delivery.

Import duty rates vary depending on the type of item ordered. For instance: Fine crystal is taxed at 7.1 percent of the foreign price, fine china is taxed at 10.4 percent, perfume is taxed at about 6 percent and gold jewelry and watches are about 7.2 percent.

You can call the import specialist at the customs department at the post office to get the exact classification and rate of duty on your desired item. It is the classification of the item that determines its rate. For example: Is the Chinese carved-wood screen classified as furniture or a work of art? The duty on a work of art is much lower.

If you feel the duty charged was not correct you can file a protest within ninety days. Send a copy of the mail-entry receipt (customs form 3419), which is on the package, plus a letter, to the customs office at the address shown on the left side of the form. If they authorize a total refund of the duty, the postal-handling fee will also be refunded.

Another procedure, when you question the duty charges, would be not to accept the parcel. Within thirty days, you would then have to provide a written statement of your objections to the charges to the postmaster at the office where the parcel is being held. Your letter will then be forwarded to the issuing customs office and your shipment will be held at the post office until a reply is received. In our experience duty has been less than we expected, often much less.

The following items may not be imported into this country:

> Most agricultural products
> Anything made from an endangered species
> Narcotics
> Poisons
> Some liquor-filled candies and absinthe
> Books, records or cassettes violating copyright laws
> Obscene articles and publications
> Seditious and treasonable materials

Lottery tickets
Products made by forced labor

For additional information you may write for customs leaflets to: U.S. Customs, P.O. Box 7407, Washington, D.C. 20044, or call (202) 566-8195.

What Is VAT?

Many responses will mention VAT. This stands for Value Added Tax and often runs as much as 25 percent. This tax is *deducted* from the price when goods are shipped out of the country. For example: Three Waterford crystal items were quoted at 131.67 pounds,

less 25.92 percent VAT . . . . . . − 34.13 pounds
_____
97.54
postage, packing and ins . . . . + 19.35 pounds
_____
your cost in Irish pounds . . . . 116.89.

Sometimes the Value Added Tax will be called by another name such as turnover tax or export tax.

What If It's Damaged?

You probably will never have to worry about this, but what if it is damaged? First notify the company by mail and wait for instructions. If it is convenient, it is a good idea to send a picture showing the damage. Keep the original package, packing material and all related papers or forms until you receive a reply.

Sometimes the company will simply send you a replacement.

If the company asks you to return the item and you have paid any duty and the postal-handling fee, write to the customs office shown on the left side of the mail-entry receipt (CF 3419), which is pasted on the package, and include with your letter evidence from the post office to show that the article has been returned. Keep a copy of all receipts and correspondence. Make sure to mark your package "Merchandise for Exchange" when returning an item.

One time something came chipped and the company gave us a merchandise credit for the amount of our return postage. We then used this toward another purchase.

Parlez-vous français?

Occasionally you may receive a reply written in a language other than English. Don't panic. Many sales and postal terms are very similar to the English terms and the form in which the letter is written will give you context clues.

We have noted those few stores that responded to our inquiries in that country's native tongue. Don't let this stop you. The store understood your inquiry well enough to answer, didn't it?

What Not to Do

As a general rule *try not to send to one country for products made in another*. For instance, order your French china from France, your Lladro from Spain and your Waterford from Ireland. Sometimes a general gift catalog will offer you the convenience of not having to write to many countries, but be aware that this method may not give you the best prices.

Some things such as cameras and electronic equipment are, surprisingly enough, cheaper in the United States in cities like New York.

Do not order directly from this book, even if you see exactly what you want with price and shipping charges given. All prices are given as references only, so that you can get an idea of what you may be able to save. Remember, merchandise and prices change, and currency fluctuates! Even while we were writing this book, prices were changing.

If you just want to browse, send to places like Cash & Company, Fallers, Emerald, Icemart and Saxkjaers that have a general mail-order catalog. Please do not send to individual stores if you are not serious about making a purchase, as catalogs, brochures and postage can become so expensive for the merchant that he will stop dealing with mail requests.

Getting Your Package from There to Here

Be sure to specify that you want your package sent by *mail*, if possible, either airmail or sea mail. If a freight-forwarding company is used, instead of a postal-handling fee of $2.50 you will have a freight-forwarding fee that may be $20.00 or $30.00 for a small package and the package will come with a C.O.D. charge from the freight-forwarding company.

However, there are times when freight forwarding may be necessary if you do not live near a port of entry for large and heavy items such as furniture and rugs. Whether or not you are picking up the item yourself, you must specify that the item be sent to the port of entry closest to where you live. This will minimize the freight-forwarding charges. If you live near a port of entry you may specify that you will pick up the item at the port yourself and that all the necessary papers are to be sent to you at home.

A note about timing: We have received packages sent airmail in as little as five days from the time of mailing and have waited from six to twelve weeks for things sent surface mail.

A Final Word

Buying the best for less is much easier than it seems and lots of fun. We have listed all the rules and regulations and possible problems so that you will know how to deal with them *if* they ever arise. In actuality, problems do not generally occur. Merchandise usually comes undamaged, in a timely fashion, and best of all with very little duty to pay—or perhaps none at all.

Blankets

WHETHER YOU LIKE SNUG-gling under down comforters or wool blankets, in your favorite chair or in a king-size bed, these are the stores to write to in order to stave off winter chills.

St. Patrick's Down
St. Patrick's Mills
Douglas, Cork
Ireland
Telephone: (011-353-21) 931 110

Comforters of 100 percent goose down, 100 percent duck down and feather/down combinations in all sizes.

Pillows in feather and down combinations.

Comforter and pillow cover sets in many colors and color combinations.

Wool mattress covers: A 2-inch layer of batted wool encased in pure cotton insulates you from underneath; your sheet goes on top.

Irish linens for the table, bed and bath.

Clothing: down jackets and vests.

A catalog with prices is available. Postage is additional. Comforters have a unique honeycomb structure with internal walls so that the down stays in place and gives even warmth. For those who want the very best, a queen-size, 100 percent goose-down comforter with a 45-ounce filling weight is $198.00 plus $15.00 airmail postage. A similar comforter in an American catalog is $289.00 plus tax and shipping.

A queen-size wool mattress cover is $75.00 plus $14.00 postage, compared to $109.00 plus tax locally.

Personal checks, bank drafts, money orders and credit cards are accepted.

Tidstrand
CH-1936 Verbier 2
Switzerland
Telephone: (011-41-26) 7 60 30
Telex: 473220

Blankets of 100 percent pure new wool.

We received thirteen fabric samples varying from brilliant rainbow hues to subtle earth tones; all are tone on tone. Tidstrand has been producing these luxurious blankets for over ninety years and they are sure to keep you cozy on the coldest of nights.

Prices are given in both Swiss francs and U.S. dollars.

An 88-by-95-inch blanket (queen/king) is 260 Swiss francs, approximately $121 at the time we received the response. Airmail postage for one blanket is approximately $25.00.

The company will accept payment by check.

For more blankets, *see*

> Brown Thomas & Co.
> Cleo, Ltd.
> Emerald
> Fallers, Ltd.
> Icemart
> Illum
> Illums Bolighus
> Irish Cottage Industries, Ltd.
> Shannon Mail Order
> St. Andrews Woolen Mill
> Tartan Gift Shop
> W. Bill, Ltd.

Books

Everything you could possibly want to know can be found in a book. Here are some places to start on your quest.

W. & G. Foyle, Ltd.
113-119 Charing Cross Road
London WC2H OEB
England
Telephone: (011-44-1) 437 5660

Books, books and more books.

Foyle's is one of the largest bookstores in the world, with a stock of over four million volumes. There is no mail-order catalog, as books quickly go out of print, but the store is more than willing to try to supply any book that you have trouble finding at home.

Postage and packing are additional and range from approximately $1.50 to $3.50 depending on the price of the volume.

For more books, *see*

Antartex, Ltd.
Anything Left Handed, Ltd.
Cash & Company, Ltd.
Emerald
Fallers, Ltd.
Force 4, Chandlery
Hamleys of Regent Street, Ltd.
Harrods
Icemart
Sogetsu School
Walton's

Cameras and
Optical Equipment

Picture these sources for your photographic needs. Note that many of the following are in the United States. Our comparisons show that this is one category in which you can do as well at home as you can abroad.

Wherever you finally buy your equipment, make sure that you get a U.S. warranty!

Bi-Rite Photo & Electronics
15 East 30th Street
New York, N.Y. 10016-7031
U.S.A.
Telephone: (212) 685-2130*

Cameras, lenses and photo accessories: Olympus, Nikon, Ricoh, Canon, Hasselblad, Minolta, Pentax, Yashica, Contax, Vivitar and Polaroid. Gossen light meters.
  Binoculars: Bushnell, etc.

Typewriters, calculators, computers, etc.

Audio components, VCRs, etc.
  Telephone systems.

Microwave ovens.

There is no catalog but you can see the ad every Sunday in the *New York Times* and also in photography magazines. There is a toll-free phone number for orders only (*1-800-223-1970). There is a minimum order of $60.00 when you use a credit card. The minimum charge for shipping and handling is $5.95. The store is open Sundays, closed Saturdays.

Checks and credit cards are accepted.

Focus Cameras
4421 13th Avenue
Brooklyn, New York 11219
U.S.A.
Telephone: (718) 436-6262*

Cameras, lenses and accessories: Minolta, Canon, Nikon, Olympus, Pentax, Yashica, Vivitar, etc.
  Binoculars.
  Projectors.

There is no catalog but you can see the ads every Sunday in the *New York Times* and in photo magazines. There is an 800 number (*1-800-221-0828) for orders only. Shipping and handling are additional. The store is open Sundays, closed Saturdays.

Checks and credit cards are accepted.

47th Street Photo
36 East 19th Street
Mail-Order Department
New York, N.Y. 10003
U.S.A.
Telephone: (212) 398-1410*

Cameras, lenses and photo accessories: Nikon, Canon, Olympus, Pentax, Minolta, Mamiya, Fuji, Hanimex, Ricoh, Omega, Vivitar, etc.
  Darkroom supplies.
  Movie and slide projectors.
  Binoculars, telescopes, etc.: Nikon, Celestron, etc.

Audio equipment and VCRs.
  Telephones and answering machines.

Typewriters, calculators, computers, printers, etc.

Microwave ovens.

Seiko watches.

You can see the ads in the *New York Times* and in photo magazines; and in addition, there is a catalog. The store has an 800 phone number (*1-800-221-7774) for ordering and there is also a Used Merchandise and Trade-In hotline (212-302-0138). For an updated list of what is available you can send a stamped, self-addressed envelope to the Used Dept. at 67 W. 47th Street, New York, N.Y. 10036.
  The store is closed on Saturdays, open on Sundays. Checks and credit cards are accepted.

Gotte
Bahnhofstrasse 98
8023 Zurich
Switzerland
Telephone: (011-41-1) 211 3780
Telex: 812414

Binoculars, monoculars, telescopes, microscopes and optical equipment by Swarovski, Weso, Zeiss, etc.

The reply we received was in German. Brochures written in German, with prices in Swiss francs, are available. There is an additional charge for postage and insurance of approximately $10.00 per item.

Checks are accepted.

Photo-Kohlroser
Maximiliansplatz 10
8000 Munich 2
Germany
Telephone: (011-49-89) 29 52 50

Cameras, lenses and accessories: Leica, Rolleiflex, Zeiss, etc.
Projectors.

Brochures are available. The VAT of 12 percent will be deducted. Airmail and insurance are additional.

We compared the prices we received against the prices in ads in the Sunday *New York Times*. We found that what we had asked for was cheaper in New York; however, you may want to use this source for hard-to-find items.

Checks are accepted.

Weber Photounternehmen
Geschaftsleitung
CH-6002 Lucerne 2
Switzerland
Telephone: (011-41-41) 23 35 35
Telex: CH 78195 Weber

Cameras, lenses and accessories: Leica, Rollei, etc.

Price lists in Swiss francs are available. For export deduct 16 percent of the price listed. Shipping costs and insurance are determined by the weight. A postage chart is included.

Unless you need something that is hard to find, check the New York stores listed above.

China

IF YOU'VE DROOLED OVER Dansk, wished for Wedgwood or longed for Limoges, this is your chapter. When you can pay as little as 30 to 50 percent of the U.S. list price, you can afford to indulge a little. Remember: The best prices will be found in the country of origin.

A/S Porsgrunn Porselen
Karl Johansgate 14
Oslo 1
Norway

Porcelain dinner services, coffee sets and tea sets.
  Oven-to-table ware in porcelain, able to go from freezer to regular or microwave oven, and of course it's dishwasher proof, too.

Porcelain figurines of animals and birds.

Giftware: vases, bowls, trivets, salt and pepper shakers, etc.

Collector's plates: Christmas, Mother's and Father's Days, etc.

Hand-decorated jewelry in porcelain and sterling silver: earrings, necklaces, pins and rings.

Porsgrunn was founded in 1885 and has been producing fine china since 1887. The designs and shapes go from the elegant to the everyday, from the classical to the modern. The shop even produces a set with the mountain flora of Norway. The story of each flower is printed on the underside of the plate. These are fast becoming collector's items.

The shop will also make plates to order to commemorate special events of all kinds.

There are two separate catalogs, one for china and one for jewelry.

A Christmas plate is 158 Norwegian kroner ($21.00) and the Mother's Day plate is 79 N.Kr. ($10.50). You now deduct 16⅔ percent VAT from these prices. Freight and insurance are additional. Customs rates are 11 percent of the net price, if collected.

Payment may be made by check in U.S. dollars.

Arabia Rorstrand Center
Pohjoisesplanadi 25
00100 Helsinki 10
Finland
Telephone: (011-358-0) 17 0055

Oven-to-table ware in modern Scandinavian-type designs.
  Ceramic cookware.

Glasses and barware.
  Glass dishes and serving pieces.

Gift items: punch bowls, ladles, ashtrays, Christmas tree ornaments, unusual glass napkin rings, salt and pepper shakers, candleholders, hurricane and oil lamps.

Vases: opaline and clear glass in blown, pressed, cut and etched styles.

Art glass: paperweights, flasks, goblets, bowls, figurines.

Collectibles: plates in varying design series: Christmas, Christmas brownies (elves), mother and child, presidents of Finland, Bjorn Landstrom ships and annual art scenes.

Ceramics: wall plaques, candleholders, lamps, clocks, vases, bowls, figurines, children's dishes, spice cannisters, rolling pins, Christmas cards, table lighters and ashtrays for pipes.

"Rice porcelain" bowls, coffee services, candleholders, etc.; flower and cache pots in embossed and smooth ceramics; porcelain doll kits (see remarks).

Stoneware chess sets.

All items available from this source are the very popular and well-known Arabia of Finland brand. We received china, glass and gift catalogs filled to the brim with great Scandinavian-designed items. Many of the items would make fantastic and unusual gifts. The ceramic Christmas cards, which are actually miniature plaques, would make terrific keepsakes. The shop also has three different miniature botanical series, gift boxed in sets of six, which could be used for hors d'oeuvres or bread and butter plates.

The doll kit is another special gift idea. The kit contains a ceramic head (boy or girl) and shoes, a pattern for the body and patterns for outfits. You can give the kit, as is, to a do-it-yourselfer or present someone special with a fully dressed doll. Equally special is the stoneware chess set and board with built-in drawers to house the modern chess pieces.

The Finnish turnover tax (VAT) of 16 percent is deducted from the price. Postage charges are additional and are determined by weight. Telephone orders are accepted with a valid credit card.

Bing & Grondahl
Amagertorv 4
1160 Copenhagen
Denmark
Telephone: (011-45-1) 12 26 86

China and stoneware dinner services, from the elegant "Offenbach" to the rustic "Rune" patterns; there are thirty-two patterns in all.
Coffee and tea services.

Figurines in both porcelain and stoneware: puppy dogs to polar bears, children at play, people at work, etc.

Gift items: trays, plaques, vases, etc., with typical Danish scenes in the famous Bing & Grondahl blue tones.

Collectibles: Mother's Day and Christmas plates, Christmas bells, doll of the year, thimbles, etc.

The items available are all Bing & Grondahl brand. Giftware and china catalogs are available. Prices on the included lists are quoted in Danish kroner, and include the Danish purchase tax (VAT), which will be deducted. Postage and insurance are additional.

We received prices in U.S. dollars on their new

"Tropical" line of giftware as seen in a popular American magazine. The 10¾-inch tray, which sells in the U.S. for $75.00, could be had for $39.00 including the shipping and insurance charges. The 3½-inch "Tropical" bon bon bowl with lid was quoted at $14.00 complete, compared with $25.00 plus tax locally.

Payment by check will be accepted.

**Cambet
10, rue de la Charité
69002 Lyon
France
Telephone: (011-33-7) 837 5677
Telex: 375 879**

*China: Bernardaud, Ceralene, Haviland, Raynaud, Coquet, Lafarge and Hermès.
    Earthenware by Atelier de Segries.*

Crystal stemware and gift items: Baccarat, Daum, Lalique, St. Louis and Sèvres.

*Silverplate by Christofle and Ercuis.
    Sterling silver by Puiforcat.*

*Furniture by Mailfert: reproductions of eighteenth-century chairs, armchairs, desks, chests of drawers, etc.
    Lamps.*

This fine china and crystal shop is really three shops: traditional tabletop items, contemporary tabletop items and furniture. The company has been in business since 1820 in the same location and is an excellent place to outfit your table and accessorize your home.

Brochures are available for most brands, and there is a worldwide shipping service.

Checks in French francs, Visa, MasterCard and American Express are accepted.

Monsieur Cambet was pleased to note that he had just opened a store, Mazza Gallerie, in Washington, D.C., telephone (202) 244-4422.

Chinacraft of London, Ltd.
Park House
130 Barlby Road
London W10 6BW
England
Telephone: (011-44-1) 960 2121 Ext. 222
Telex: 923550

Fine china and earthenware: Aynsley, Coalport, Johnson Brothers, Minton, Royal Albert, Royal Crown Derby, Royal Doulton, Royal Worcester, Spode, Wedgwood, etc.

Crystal: Royal Brierly, Stuart, Edinburgh of Scotland, Tyrone, Waterford, Baccarat, etc.

Giftware: Royal Doulton character and toby jugs, figurines, etc.; Coalport "cottages"; various brands of china floral bouquets.

Royal Doulton's "Bunnykins" pattern, Wedgwood's "Peter Rabbit" and "Paddington" patterns; and for the child in all of us, miniature tea sets by Wedgwood in some of the most popular patterns.

Solid brass carriage clocks.

Our price comparisons show that you can save from 50 to 70 percent dealing with this firm. We received a delivered price of $320 for four five-piece place settings of Royal Doulton's "Carlyle" pattern, which lists for $168.00 for one *four*-piece place setting in the U.S.

Wedgwood's "Runnymede" pattern was $240.00 for four five-piece place settings, delivered. Sale price at home was $585.00, plus sales tax, for the same twenty pieces.

This company, which has thirty-five showrooms and stores, has been in business over thirty years. It carries a complete line of English and European china and crystal. However, the best buys will be on English-made goods. We have dealt with this company in person, by mail and by phone, and have always been completely satisfied. Each year you will be notified when representatives are coming to the States and you can arrange to see the merchandise they bring or you can speak to them on the phone to obtain a price quote.

Personal checks, money orders and charge cards are accepted.

Csemege-Hungarian Intertourist Shops
P.O. Box 482
1053 Budapest 5, Szep Utca 6
Hungary
Telephone: (011-36-1) 173-211
Telex: 22-65924

China dinnerware: Herend, Hollohaza and Zsolnay.

Figurines: Herend and Hollohaza.

One of Hungary's most famous exports is Herend china. If you are familiar with Herend china, you know the patterns are beautiful and the serving and accessory pieces are exquisite.

There is an Intertourist catalog which is of absolutely no help, but the store will respond to your inquiry with a detailed letter, and in English, too.

If you can get a picture of the pattern or figurine of your choice, send it, as pattern names may differ from the ones you see in the stores here. Be sure to inquire whether your pattern is in stock, otherwise it may take over a year until it is available. Of course, for savings like these, we're willing to wait.

The prices we compared showed a saving of 60 to 70 percent, and they were quoted in U.S. dollars. Packing, sea freight and insurance for a set of china is about $100.00.

Checks and credit cards are accepted.

> **Editions Paradis**
> **29, rue de Paradis**
> **75010 Paris**
> **France**
> **Telephone: (011-33-1) 4523 0534**

China dinnerware: Bernardaud, Ceralene, Haviland, Haviland Limoges, etc.

Crystal stemware and giftware: Baccarat, St. Louis, Sèvres, Daum, etc.

Silver: Cristofle, etc.

Rue de Paradis is lined with shops filled with china and crystal. We were taken to this particular shop by Sylvain and Celyna, Parisian friends of ours, when we told them that we were looking for a new set of china.

The store does not have a catalog; however, all French brands of merchandise are available for the bride-to-be as well as the rest of us. There is a VAT discount of about 16 percent. Insurance and shipping are additional but considerably less than the VAT discount.

We bought Bernardaud's "Artois" service for ten, including soup bowls, plus a tea pot, covered vegetable dish, gravy boat and a large serving platter for about 7,000 francs. (This was about $735.00. At the time the dollar was at its strongest.) This price included shipping and insurance. The same pieces at home totaled approximately $1,700.00 plus tax. All the pieces arrived in perfect condition. Duty on our purchase was a whopping $10.65 plus $2.50 for the postal-collection fee.

Just to check out our source by mail, we wrote to inquire about Ceralene's "Lafayette" pattern. It was $85.00 for one five-piece place setting compared to $145.00 for the same thing at home. Their price quote showed the VAT deduction and the shipping and insurance charges so that we were aware of the complete cost. We were also told that there would be a three-month delay on this pattern. We think the savings are worth the wait.

The English Shop
Market Square
P.O. Box 1080
St. Thomas
U.S. Virgin Islands 00801
Telephone: 1-800-524-2013
Telex: 3470119

China: Arzberg, Bernardaud, Bing & Grondahl, Ceralene, Coalport, Denby, Duchess Bone China, Franciscan, Richard Ginori, Hammersley, Haviland, Heinrich, Johnson Brothers, Kaiser, Mason, Minton, Paragon, Portmeirion, Royal Albert, Royal Doulton, Royal Grafton, Royal Worcester, Spode, Villeroy & Boch, and Wedgwood.

Crystal stemware and giftware: Barthmann, Bayel, Cavan, Dema, Gobel, Riedel, Royal Brierly, St. Louis, Stuart, Swarovski, Val St. Lambert, Vannes Le Chatel and Wittwer.

Figurines in wood, crystal and porcelain: Anri, Belleek, Beswick, Bing & Grondahl, Bossons' heads, Capodimonte, Coalport, Irish Dresden, Nao by Lladro, Reijmyre and Royal Doulton.

Watches: They are an authorized Seiko dealer.

This company, which has a small brochure, says that it is the only shop in St. Thomas that guarantees 35 to 50 percent savings on china and crystal. They are happy to accept your mail or phone order. Notice the *toll-free* phone number. Shipping, insurance and customs duty comes to less than 10 percent of your total bill.

The Bossons' head of a chef was $16.00 including shipping charges. It is currently selling for $24.00 plus tax locally. The "Artois" pattern of Bernardaud china was $69.00 here for a five-piece place setting.

Checks and credit cards are accepted.

Focke & Meltzer
P. C. Hoofstraat 65-67
Amsterdam
Holland
Telephone: (011-31-20) 642 311
Telex: 38207

China: Royal Delft, Makkum, Herend, Meissen, Rosenthal, Royal Copenhagen and Wedgwood.

Royal Leerdom crystal stemware and giftware.

Christofle silver.

Giftware: authentic De Porceleyne Fles, "Blue and White Delftware," ginger jars, vases, temple jars, candlesticks, decanters, figurines, shoes, plates, clocks and ashtrays.

Authentic blue and multicolored Royal Makkum ware: plates, bowls, small dishes, cache pots, vases, figurines, candlesticks, serving plates, cannisters and ginger jars.

Brochures with price lists are available. This is a high-quality gift shop that specializes in authentic Delft and Makkum ware and Dutch-made Royal Leerdom glass. It also carries fine quality merchandise from most other European countries.

Personal checks are accepted.

**Gmunder Keramik
Johannes Hohenberg KG
Keramikstrasse 24-P.O. 232
A-4810 Gmunden
Austria
Telephone: (011-43-7612) 5441 Serie**

Ceramic dinnerware and coordinating giftware and accessories: umbrella stands, mirror frames, spice sets, punch-bowl sets, soup tureens, rum pots, salt box, piggy banks, candlesticks, baskets, beer steins, figurines, crucifixes, religious plaques, holy water containers and advent rings.

A black-and-white catalog with photographs of the basic pieces is available, along with a color brochure showing the pieces finished in the available patterns. Most of the accessories can be made to match whichever china pattern you choose, so you can coordinate them.

We saw some of these charming pieces in Tiffany's recently. Price lists are in Austrian schillings and include packing. Shipping is additional.

Checks are accepted.

**Michael Kuchenreuther
Sonnenstrasse 22
8000 Munich 2
Germany
Telephone: (011-49-89) 594 525**

China dinnerware and gifts: Furstenberg, Hutschenreuther, Rosenthal Studio-Line, Kaiser, KPM (Royal Porcelain Manufactury), Goebel and others.

Handcut glass and crystal stemware and barware.

Figurines by Hummel, Goebel, etc.

We found an ad for this store in a hotel magazine that J.B. brought back from his latest trip to Germany and Austria. We immediately wrote and asked for the Hummel "Umbrella Girl," which sells for $300.00 here. The price was DM 449.00 ($201.00), plus about $15.00 postage and insurance.

This store exports to all countries and carries all the china and glass you need to set a beautiful table.

Payment by money order is accepted.

> **Nymphenburg Porzellan**
> **Odeonplatz 1**
> **8000 Munich 22**
> **Germany**
> **Telephone: (011-49-89) 28 24 28**

China dinner services, fish services, coffee and tea services, and soup tureens.

Nymphenburg porcelain figurines.

Giftware: candelabra, open-worked china baskets and vases, cache pots, boxes and beer steins.

For over two hundred years Nymphenburg porcelain has been made and decorated by hand. Because it is still completely handmade your order will take approximately six to eight months to complete, but it is worth the wait. The patterns range from the rococo to more contemporary styles and are shown in the illustrated brochures which come complete with price lists in German marks. Insurance, packing and postage are approximately 10 percent additional.

Checks are accepted.

Reject China Shops
33-35 Beauchamp Place
London SW3 1NU
England
Telephone: (011-44-1) 581 0733

China and ceramics: Adams, Aynsley, Bernardaud, Burgess & Leigh, Caverswall, Coalport, Denby, Haviland, Masons, Gien, Hornsea, Johnson Brothers, Midwinter, Palissy, Paragon, Poole Pottery, Portmeirion, Royal Albert, Royal Grafton, Royal Worcester, Spode, T. G. Green and Villeroy & Boch.

Crystal stemware and giftware: Atlantis, Baccarat, Daum, Edinburgh, St. Louis, Stuart, Tyrone, Waterford and Webb Corbett.

Giftware: Hummel, Lalique crystal, Royal Doulton dolls, Coalport "Ladies of Fashion" and "Cottages," Paddington Bear, Aynsley china bouquets, Belleek, Royal Worcester "Evesham" table accessories, Price & Kensington Cottageware, I.C.T.C. Italian cookware and serving pieces and Portmeirion "Botanic Garden" tabletop accessories.

Spode "Christmas Tree" table accessories.

Every time we go to London we stop in at least one of these stores to see what's new. They're right near Harrods' department store.

A catalog is available for $3.00. While the name says Reject, most of the merchandise is first quality. The store stocks a much larger range of items than is listed in the catalog, so if it is not listed, an inquiry would be in order. Prices, given in U.S. dollars, include postage and insurance when you order a minimum of four place settings of china or a minimum of eight glasses; otherwise, there is a $10.00 charge. The store has a direct gift service which will gladly send your gift to the happy recipient.

A five-piece place setting of Spode's "Fleur de Lys" is $80.45 compared to $230.00 here. Even on sale the price was $161.00 per place setting locally. Most other patterns we compared averaged approximately a 50 percent saving.

The small Baccarat "Harmonie" vase is $34.00 compared to $65.00 locally.

Our price comparisons on Hummel figurines showed that the few dollars saved would be wiped out by the postage charges.

Credit cards and international money orders in pounds sterling are accepted.

Rosenthal Studio-Haus
Konigstrasse 5
8500 Nurenberg 1
Germany
Telephone (011-49-911) 22 18 61

China dinnerware and oven-to-table ware by Rosenthal, Arabia of Finland, Dansk and Thomas.

Crystal stemware, barware and giftware by Rosenthal, iittala of Finland, Riedel, Kosta Boda, Orrefors, etc.

Flatware and hollow ware in sterling, silver plate and gold plate by Rosenthal and Pott.

Cookware and kitchenware by Stelton of Denmark and Spring of Switzerland.

Collectibles: Rosenthal Christmas plates, "Opera" china and figurines and other limited art editions.

Toys: creative wooden toys from Switzerland.

Brochures are available, some in English and some in German. Only some brochures came with price lists so a second letter may be necessary. If your request is specific, the store will reply with a price that includes shipping and insurance charges. The reply even converted deutschemarks into dollars for us.

Payment may be made by personal check or credit card.

Standing Decors 2
21 bis, rue de Paradis
75010 Paris
France
Telephone: (011-33-1) 4246 2982

China: Bernardaud, Ceralene, Haviland, etc.

Crystal stemware and giftware: Baccarat, Daum, St. Louis, Sèvres, etc.

When the Baccarat store was out of the candlesticks one of our daughters wanted to buy, this was where she made her purchase. The price was the same as it was at the Baccarat store.

We wrote to check on the price of the medium- and large-size Baccarat vases in the "Harmonie" pattern. The shop responded quickly with a letter giving us prices in both francs and dollars. The price was $71.00 compared to $130.00 for the medium size and $213.00 compared to $370.00 for the large size. Postage and insurance are additional.

The price on Ceralene's "Dioraflor" pattern showed a 23 percent saving even after postage and insurance were added.

Bank checks are accepted.

Steigerwald
Residenzstrasse 19-20
8000 Munich 2
Germany
Telephone: (011-49-89) 224 200

China dinnerware, coffee and tea sets: Meissen, Horchst, Augarten (Weiner Porzellanmanufaktur), KPM (Royal Porcelain Manufactory), Hutschenreuther, Fursten-burg, Heinrich, Villeroy & Boch, Arzberg, Kaiser, Her-end and others.

Crystal and glass stemware and barware: Josephinen-hutte, Theresienthal Bavaria, Markus von Freyberg, Villeroy & Boch, Nachtmann and Christinenhutte.
Crystal chandeliers by Palwa.

Flatware and hollow ware: Wilkens, Robbe & Berking, Hanauer Silberschmiede and others.

Figurines: Hummel, Meissen, KPM, Hochst, Sitzendorf, Augarten, Hutschenreuther, Kaiser, Goebel, etc.

Giftware: Meissen vases, ginger jars, candlesticks and candelabra, compotes, candy dishes, jewelry, etc.; Dresden china vases, urns, soup tureens, decorative plates, etc.; Plaue Porzellan end tables; silver- and gold-plated tabletop accessories; crystal candlesticks; placemats, framed miniatures, cruet sets and wine coolers; Belgian pewter steins, trays, wall plaques, wine coolers, etc.

Christmas and religious items: crèches figures, etc., by Hutschenreuther and Goebel; Heinrich porcelain icons.

Our friend Gerlinde, who lives near Munich, reports that this store, in business for over 150 years, is a place to shop for Hummel figurines, china, giftware, etc.

Of course we wrote. We received a postcard written in English, followed the next day by a catalog in German. After you have made your selection from this extensive catalog, a second letter will be needed to obtain prices and shipping information.

Thomas Goode & Co., Ltd.
Att: Mail-Order Department
19 South Audley Street
London W1Y 6BN
England
Telephone: (011-41-1) 499-2823

China dinnerware: Aynsley, Coalport, Minton, Royal Albert, Royal Crown Derby, Royal Doulton, Royal Worcester, Spode, Wedgwood and other European brands.

Crystal stemware and barware: Royal Brierley, Tudor, Stuart, Edinburgh of Scotland, Waterford, etc.

Giftware: Dubarry porcelain desk items, vases, covered boxes; Christofle silver-plated accessories; travel clocks.
   Wine coolers, vodka and caviar sets, crystal ashtrays, decanters, trays, etc.

This is a fine china and glass shop with the facilities for producing crested and monogrammed dinner services and glassware. In addition to china and crystal, it carries silverware, antique decanters, chandeliers and giftware. A catalog showing some of the gift items is available.
   Prices in the gift catalog include shipping and insurance and the VAT has been deducted.
   International money orders and credit cards are accepted. A surcharge of $15.00 is made if you use a personal check.

Vista Alegre
Largo Barao de Quintela, 3
1200 Lisbon
Portugal
Telephone: (011-351-1) 32 80 81
Telex: 16722 Valis P

China dinnerware and serving pieces.

This fine porcelain is not seen too often in the United States, although we did see it in a New York department store. It has been produced in Portugal for about 150 years and can be found in many of their museums.

The store has both traditional and contemporary designs, and a series of brochures showing a variety of patterns is available. Be sure to ask that a price list be included.

If for any reason you have the need to call, we have been in the store and the personnel speak English.

Zoellner-Rosenthal Porzellanhaus
Theatinerstrasse 8
D-8000 Munich 2
Germany
Telephone: (011-49-89) 22 04 22

China dinnerware and oven-to-table ware in Rosenthal's various styles, from the traditional to the modern "Studio" line.

Rosenthal crystal stemware, barware and giftware.

Rosenthal silver plate, gold plate and sterling silver flatware.

Collector's plates.

Giftware: vases, ashtrays, smoking sets, wall plaques, candleholders and covered bon bon dishes.

This store carries only the Rosenthal brand and is geared for the mail-order business. Dr. Zoellner claims you will save at least 40 percent of U.S. prices. After you choose the pattern from the many brochures he sends, tell him which pieces you want and he will send you a price quote including insurance and postage charges.

Checks are accepted.

For more china, *see*

A. B. Nordiska Kompaniet
A. B. Schou
A. H. Riise Gift Shops
Alois Dallmayr
Art et Sélection, s.p.r.l.
Brown Thomas & Co.
C. J. Josephssons Glas & Porslin AB
Cash & Co., Ltd.
China Products Co. (H.K.), Ltd.
Chinese Arts & Crafts, Ltd.
Christofle
Chung Kiu Chinese Prod. Emporium
Den Kongelige Porcelain Factory
Den Permanente A/S
E. Bakalowits Sohne GmbH
Emerald
Fallers, Ltd.
Galeries Lafayette
The General Trading Co., Ltd.
Harrods
Illum
Illums Bolighus
Little Switzerland
Lobmeyr
Magasin
OY Stockmann AB
Roittner
Saxkjaers
Scandinavian Center
Shannon Mail Order
Takashimaya
Yue Hwa Chinese Prod. Emporium

Christmas and Religious Items

FAMILY CHRISTMAS TRADI-
tions start here. Crèche figures and nativity sets, tree
ornaments, Christmas spoons and china, et cetera,
can all be sent for.

Religious furnishings for the church are also available by mail.

===

Al Pellegrino Cattòlico
Via di Porta Angelica, 83
00193 Rome
Italy
Telephone: (011-39-6) 654 2351

*Rosaries made of wood, rose petals, crystal, enamel,
mother-of-pearl, semiprecious stones, filigree, etc. Rosaries in metal, sterling silver and gold-filled settings.*

*Statues in porcelain, imitation white marble, hand-carved
wood, etc.*

*Mosaics, religious articles for the church and home,
records, etc.*

All religious articles can be blessed by the Pope at no
extra charge.

There is no catalog, but if you describe what you want, Mrs. Corinaldesi will send you descriptions of what is available. The prices are given in U.S. dollars. Rosaries in sterling silver start at $14.00. Statues of the madonna start at $10.00.

Certified checks are accepted.

China Handicraft Co., Ltd.
No. 21 Lock Road, 1st floor
Kowloon
Hong Kong
Telephone: (011-852-3) 669 406

Religious articles: hand-carved ivory and teak-wood statues in both Caucasian and Oriental styles; hand-painted silk religious paintings.
  Ivory rosaries and medals.

Jewelry: pearl necklaces, earrings, rings and clasps; lapis and other semiprecious stone necklaces, cufflinks, earrings and rings.

Oriental furniture and carved chests.

Giftware: Oriental curios and novelties, porcelain tableware, embroidered pictures.

Objets d'art: precious-stone carvings.

Fabric: silk by the yard.

This listing comes to us by way of our editor Rosann's brother, Father Anthony Ward.

Brochures with price lists are available. A 20-inch handmade ivory rosary with silver chain is $46.00. Carvings start at $85.00.

China Handicrafts has its own ivory-carving workshop and, if you don't see what you want, will make carvings from your designs or models.

Payment accepted by personal check or bank draft. If you visit the shop in person, you can use credit cards. If you are ordering jewelry, the store will pay the postage.

Karl Storr
Kaufingerstrasse 25
8000 Munich 2
Germany
Telephone: (011-49-89) 22 95 14

Hand-carved crèche figures and crèches in natural or painted wood in two sizes: 12 and 15 cm (6 inches and 7½ inches).

Brochures and price lists are available for each size. Prices include the VAT, which will be deducted from export orders. These beautiful figures are sure to become family heirlooms.

The price of a 12cm decorated Mary or Joseph is 158 deutschemarks ($65.00) each, less the VAT. The infant Jesus in a basket is 86 deutschemarks, ($34.00), less the VAT. The large sizes are slightly more.

Checks are accepted.

S. Baltinester
40 Jaffa Rd.
Zion Square
Jerusalem
Israel
Telephone: (011-972-2) 233 578

Religious items: sterling-silver menorahs, candlesticks, mezuzas, kiddush cups and plates and torah pointers.
   Sterling talit clips.
   Brass candlesticks and mezuzas.
   Yarmulkes.

Gold jewelry: Judaica pendants and earrings; personal name pendants, earrings, necklaces, rings and bracelets in either Hebrew or English; enamel bracelets.

A catalog with prices in U.S. dollars is available for a $3.00 charge. One thing that caught our eye was a 10-by-8½-inch menorah, available in either bronze or silver plate, that converts from a straight kosher menorah into various shapes. It seems very well priced at $58.00 plus $10.00 shipping.
   Payment is accepted by check or money order.

> **Talleres de Arte Grande, S.A.**
> **Serrano, 56**
> **Madrid 1**
> **Spain**
> **Telephone: (011-34-1) 275 9015**

Religious articles: chalices, crucifixes, crowns, bells, plaques and statues, holy water fonts, lavabos, candelabra, candleholders, candle snuffers, reliquaries, altar pieces, tryptics, wafer containers, book stands, etc.

This firm has been making articles for the Church since 1891. The catalog contains a large selection, but nowhere near all of what it produces. The price list is in pesetas and the items are described in Spanish, but the catalog, filled with photographs and style numbers, makes ordering easy. Items are made of silver or gilded silver, some with beautiful enamel work.

You can also order custom work to your specifications.

You must deduct 13 percent VAT from the prices listed. Postage and packing are additional.

The firm accepts checks, postal money orders and charge cards.

Tiroler Heimatwerk
Meranerstrasse 2
6020 Innsbruck
Austria
Telephone: (011-43-5222) 22 3 20

Religious and Christmas: tree decorations of wood and glass; wood carvings of saints, madonnas, crèche figures and mangers.

Tyrolian and eastern Alpine handmade folkcraft: blown, engraved and hand-painted glassware; ceramic kitchen and dinnerware; pewter, wood and wrought-iron items.
  Spinning wheels; dolls in native dress.
  Rag rugs and handwoven carpets.

Fabrics and yarns.

Table linens.

Silver and garnet jewelry.

Clothing: custom tailoring of folk costumes, dirndls and accessories for men and women. Wedding dirndls are available, and hand-knit sweaters, mittens, gloves and hats.

This is a cooperative dedicated to the preservation of a culture. The catalog touches on the many kinds of items made. After you receive the catalog you must then write a second letter for more details.

For more Christmas and religious items, *see*

A. B. Schou
Alois Dallmayr
Arabia Rorstrand Center
Cash & Co., Ltd.
China Products Co. (H.K.), Ltd.
Den Permanente A/S
Fallers, Ltd.
Franz Roozen
The General Trading Co., Ltd.
Georg Jensen Silver
Gmunder Keramik
Illum
OY Stockmann AB
Saxkjaers
Scandinavian Center
Shannon Mail Order
Steigerwald

Clothing

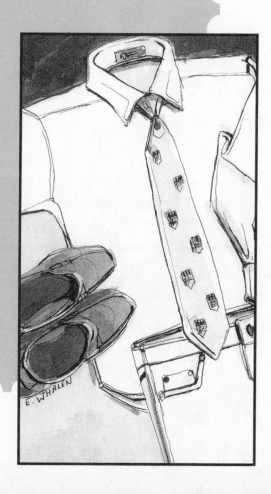

E. WHALEN

Looking like a million doesn't have to cost a fortune. Burberrys' rainwear and accessories, Icelandic and British woolens, silks, and other fine fashions can be yours for a fraction of the cost at home, if you care to do your homework.

Angus
Wilton Dean
Hawick
Scotland TD9 7HX
Telephone: (011-44-450) 73 427

Clothing for men and women: sweaters and knitware in lamb's wool, shetland, cashmere and merino wool by Pringle, Smedley, Barrie, Peter Scott, Larissa, etc.
Kilts, skirts, scarves, capes, ties, umbrellas.

The Angus shop specializes in knitwear. A variety of brochures and catalogs is available and an extra nice touch is the small snips of knitted fabric samples that are included.

Prices are given in pounds sterling and include airmail postage to the United States. For example, a woman's Pringle cashmere round neck sweater is 75 pounds sterling (about $105.00).

Checks and Visa are accepted.

Antartex, Ltd.
Lomond Industrial Estate
Alexandria, Dunbartonshire
Scotland
Telephone: (011-44-3) 895 2393

Clothing: sheepskin jackets, coats, hats, mittens and slippers.
Hand-knit shetland and "Icelander" sweaters.

Sheepskin rugs.

Knitting books.

Shetland wool yarn.

This family-owned tannery has supplied sheepskin to the British and New Zealand Trans-Antarctic Survey teams for the past twenty-five years, thus the name Antartex. All coat styles can be made in curly as well as straight skins and alterations are done for a small extra charge. A size chart and price list are included with the catalog.

When we received our copy of the catalog, a note was included saying that the suede styles shown were not available due to difficulties in obtaining high-grade skins. It's worth a letter, if suede is what you are looking for, as the supply situation may have changed.

Icelander sweaters can be knit in a variety of color combinations: You have five dyed and five natural colors from which to choose. For the do-it-yourselfer there are three pattern books available specially designed for Antartex heavy knitting yarn. Also for the do-it-yourselfer are sheepskin slipper, mitten and eyeglass-case kits complete with instructions, needle and thread.

We saw hand-sewn shearling mittens and slippers for $20.00 and $25.00 locally. The comparable Antartex mittens and slippers were $7.50 and $8.25. (We deducted 13 percent VAT from the prices listed.)

Postage and packing are additional. Checks, postal money orders and charge cards are accepted.

Berk
46 Burlington Arcade
London W1
England
Telephone: (011-44-1) 493 0028

Clothing: knitware for men and women by Ballantyne, McGeorge, Barrie, etc.
Men's clothing by Chester Barrie.
Ladies' kilts, skirts, scarves, dresses and capes.
The complete line of Burberrys raincoats, rainwear and accessories.

When Burberrys was out of stock in the raincoat "hubby" wanted, the shop sent him to Berk! The prices were the same as at Burberrys.

Hubby asked whether mail orders are accepted and the answer was yes, and he got lots of brochures to take home. What we liked best in the brochures was the superb collection of cashmere clothing: not just sweaters, but skirts, dresses, capes, scarves, coats, jackets, et cetera.

Brochures, color charts and price lists are available for the asking. Prices are in pounds sterling and 13 percent VAT will be deducted. Postage and insurance are additional.

Checks or credit cards are accepted.

Burberrys
18-22 Haymarket Street
London SW1 Y 4DQ
England
Telephone: (011-44-1) 930 3343

Clothing: raincoats, wool or rayon lined, with Burberrys' distinctive plaid; also duffle coats, skirts, shirts, sweaters, and hats; scarves in wool, silk and cashmere.

Leather and leather-fabric combinations: handbags, attaché and briefcases, luggage, golf and tennis bags; slippers and shoes; toiletry cases; golf gloves.

Accessories: umbrellas, wallets, address books, belts, caps, ties, tie clips, key chains and key cases.

Giftware: desk accessories and picture frames, bridge sets, pocket flasks and traveling liquor sets, manicuring sets.

Toiletries for men.

Burberrys isn't just a coat, it's a tradition, and for a full selection of fabrics and styles you can't beat sending to the source. The rainwear brochure came with an export price list and a large number of fabric samples. The choice of fabrics and styles seems greater than what we have seen in local stores. Measurement forms were included and, of course, all merchandise is Burberrys' own brand. Savings on raincoats ran about 25 percent.

The Burberrys plaid is known the world over and shows up on just about every item, either on the inside or the outside. A cashmere scarf in the traditional Burberrys plaid retails for $75.00 locally and will cost $45.00 by mail. The accessories make great gifts and there is a separate gift and accessories catalog.

Golf originated in Scotland, and Burberrys has everything for the golfer except the clubs. If golf is your thing, ask for "The Burberrys Golf Collection" catalog.

Checks, money orders and credit cards are accepted.

Cleo, Ltd.
18 Kildare Street
Dublin
Ireland
Telephone: (011-353-1) 761 421

Clothing: Aran hand-knit sweaters for him, for her, and for the children; hats, gloves, mittens, scarves, leg warmers and shawls are also available.

Jackets and coats in tweeds and Aran knits.

Capes, cloaks, kilts, skirts and suits (for him and her).

Blankets.

Fabrics: heavyweight and lightweight tweeds by the yard or meter.

Knitting yarns in a variety of natural and dyed colors.

Many of the sweaters are made with the natural oils remaining. This makes the sweater quite waterproof. The sweaters are oatmeal in color and gradually wash to a creamy white, as the oil is washed out. A woman's heavy pullover sweater sells for about $73.00. The flecked and solid woven fabrics used in their clothing are specially woven to match the yarn colors. You can order what you want already made up or you can sew and knit your own.

The knitting yarn is a bargain at $11.50 per ½ kg. This equals 17½ ounces. We are definitely placing an order as soon as this book is done.

A measurement diagram is sent along with a brochure and a card full of fabric and yarn samples. A price list is also included. Postage and insurance are additional.

Personal checks and bank drafts are accepted; credit cards are not.

Cost-Less Clothing
317 Excelsior Hotel Shopping Center
Causeway Bay, Hong Kong
Hong Kong
Telephone: (011-852-5) 790 6815

Custom-made clothing: shirts and suits.

Cost-Less comes highly recommended by our friend J.C., who restocks his wardrobe here whenever he is in Hong Kong on business. John has only one complaint about this firm, and that's their name. He wants to know why his custom-made clothing has to have a label that says "Cost-Less." John removes the label as soon as he gets home.

We wrote to Cost-Less and asked about having shirts made to order. The store sent us eighteen fabric samples for sport and dress shirts and included an explicit measuring form and style-selection charts. There are fifteen collar styles, three long-sleeve cuffs and four short-sleeve finishes, and four shirt-front styles from which to choose. A monogram is included in the price, and there are thirty-seven design choices.

If there is something specific that you want and don't see in the choices, send a picture or sample shirt and the shop will be happy to duplicate it for you.

Dacron and cotton shirts are $18.00 each at this writing. There is a $6.00 charge for airmail postage and insurance for three shirts. There is also a $.90 charge, per order, for C.C.O. (whatever that is).

Personal checks and bank drafts are accepted.

David's Shirts, Ltd.
33 Kimberly Rd., G/F
Wing Lee Building
Kowloon
Hong Kong
Telephone: (011-852-3) 679 556

Made-to-order clothing: sport and dress shirts, pajamas and robes for men and women; men's made-to-order underwear.

Send $2.00 (which will be deducted from your first order) for this catalog, which comes complete with 218 fabric swatches and multiple measuring charts, showing you where to measure each and every part of your body, and drawings on which to indicate your general body shape.

Once you have gotten this far, you are now ready to choose from thirty-seven collar styles, twelve cuff styles, and eight pocket styles. If you like a monogram, there are forty-five styles from which to choose. If it's a tuxedo shirt you are after, you can choose from the twelve different fronts that are available. For new mail-order customers, the store prefers that you send a sample shirt that fits you perfectly.

All materials are sanforized and preshrunk before cutting. Prices start at $24.00 per shirt and are determined by the fabric you choose: Dacron and cotton, Dacron and silk, cotton, Swiss voile or pure silk. Monograms are a small additional charge.

Three shirts is the minimum number you can order and mailing charges would be $6.00. One free shirt is given with every order of eleven.

If you are a hard-to-fit size, this is the answer to your shopping problems.

Bank drafts or money orders are requested from first-time customers. Repeat customers may send their personal checks.

E. Braun & Co.
Graben 8
A 1010 Vienna
Austria
Telephone: (011-43-222) 52 55 05

Clothing: Loden coats, 70 percent wool/30 percent cashmere blend, with leather trim.

This company does not produce a catalog, but sent us two sketches and luscious fabric and leather samples in response to our inquiry. The styles are traditional Austrian styles as seen in expensive American catalogs for about $425.00. Braun's price was $265.00 and included airmail postage and insurance.

Inquire about other woolen clothing and linen which might interest you.

Checks or credit cards are accepted.

Edinburgh Woolen Mill
Langholm
Dumfriesshire
DG 13 OEB
Scotland
Telephone: (011-44-541) 80 092

Clothing for men and women: sweaters (wool, cashmere, lamb's wool, shetland, Aran and Icelandic wool); skirts, kilts, suits, jackets, blouses and vests; tweed and camel-hair jackets and coats; Icelandic hand-knit sweaters; Icelandic mountain sheep jackets and sweaters; Aran hand-knit sweaters, scarves, mittens and hats.

Yarn kits, with instructions: Aran and Icelandic.

This is a catalog put out for the first time with prices in U.S. dollars for the winter of 1985–86. It contains merchandise directly from the shop's own mills, plus a selection from Pringle of Scotland and Eider Knits. Prices look very good to us: A man's double-weight, round-neck cashmere pullover is only $99.00 plus shipping.

Sizing information and a color chart are included.

A "Club Embroidery Service" is available to put monograms, crests or insignias on pullovers.

There is a toll-free number (1-800-325-2726) to use when placing orders only. The charge for shipping your total order, by air, is only $10.00.

Personal checks, bank drafts and credit cards are accepted.

P.S.: While we were proofreading the manuscript the Summer Collection catalog arrived. There are machine-washable women's lamb's-wool sweaters in pastel colors for $22.50 and full-fashioned men's cotton pullovers for $27.50. An exceptional buy is the traditional hand-knit Aran wool round-neck pullovers in men's and women's sizes.

Force 4, Chandlery
30 Bressendam Place
Buckingham Palace Road
London SW1E 5DB
England
Telephone: (011-44-1) 828 3900/ 3382
Telex: 266003 SAFENT G

Foul-weather gear: one-piece dinghy suits, coastal suits, all-weather suits, jackets and trousers, storm smocks, float jackets, high-fit trousers, thermal underwear, children's trousers and jackets by Henri Lloyd, Musto & Hyde, Splashdown, Douglas Gill, Helen Hansen, Javlin and Puffa.

Sweaters: Guernsey sweaters and naturally waterproof fisherman's sweaters in both V- and crew-neck styles.

Caps, scarves, wallets and sailing gloves.

Skis, boots and bindings: well-known brands.

Marine hardware: wind-speed indicators, automatic tiller pilots, compasses, torch lights, winch mate vises, Curry knives and tools.
Flotation vests and sea float aids.

Books: yachting and racing handbooks, sailing books, log books, and books of general interest to the sailor.
Calendars, too.

Collapsible bicycles: Bickerton, three-speed with aluminum frame and stainless-steel fittings. Carrying bag and instruction manual are included.

Force 4 has one of the largest selections of foul-weather gear in London. The store is known for its friendly, efficient and very knowledgeable staff. Feel free to write or telex for additional information or catalogs if you have any questions. You deduct the VAT from prices given. Telephone orders are welcome.

Payment by check or credit card is accepted. Postage and packing are additional.

Highland Home Industries
53 George Street
Edinburgh EH2 3DQ
Scotland
Telephone: (011-44-31) 225 5464

Clothing: an exceptional collection of fine wool jackets, skirts, kilts and Fair Isle and Icelandic-style sweaters; hand-knit Aran sweaters, both crew neck and cardigan.
Ladies' suits.

The Clan Royal collection coordinates colors so that you can easily mix and match solids and plaids. The hand-knit Aran sweaters are particularly well priced. At this writing, a lady's sweater sells for under $60.00, including postage.

Checks and credit cards accepted.

Icemart—Mail-Order Department
Keflavik International Airport
Iceland 235
Telephone: 1-800-431-9003, to order only

Clothing: Samband shearling coats and jackets for men and women.

Icelandic wool jackets and coats for women and jackets only for men and children.

Hand-knit Lopi wool sweaters and machine-knit Icelandic sweaters.

Matching Icelandic sweater and skirt outfits for a dressier look.

Hand-knit openwork and handwoven shawls.

Icelandic ponchos, leg warmers, gloves, mittens, hats, slippers and scarves.

Blankets and lap rugs.

Yarn: 3½-ounce skeins of Lopi yarn are $3.25 and they come in shades of white, gray, brown, green, blue, pink and black, for a total of fourteen different shades.

Sweater kits with yarn and instructions included.

Dolls in Iceland's national costumes.

Books about Iceland in many languages.

There is a catalog with a size chart included. Notice there is a toll-free telephone number for your order. Prices are given in U.S. dollars and include packing, airfreight and insurance.

If you've never owned one, Icelandic wool knit coats and jackets are wonderful for the carpool life many of us lead. They are like comfortable, lined sweaters. They're lightweight but remarkably warm. A hip-length jacket with a high rolled collar is $99.00 from Icemart, and $175.00 locally. Only the design is different. You can save $102.00 on a belted, wrap coat that is almost identical to one we've seen here. (The pattern was slightly different.)

The books make excellent gifts, especially *The Visitor's Guide*, which will delight the armchair traveler.

There is also a summer catalog full of high-fashion cotton- and acrylic-blend sweaters.

Checks, credit cards and money orders are accepted.

Irish Cottage Industries, Ltd.
44 Dawson Street
Dublin 2
Ireland

Clothing: hand-knit Aran sweaters, gloves, mittens, scarves and hats for men, women and children.
 Wool stoles and shawls.
 Tweed hats, caps and ties.
 Irish linen handkerchiefs.

Tweed placemats and lap rugs.

Blackthorn walking sticks.

Collector's spoons with crests.

A brochure and price list are available. Tweed samples will be sent upon request for a $1.00 charge.

Children's Aran sweaters run about $30.00 to $35.00.

A woman's sweater is $75.00 compared to its U.S. counterpart at $135.00.

Checks are accepted.

Kathleen's
Upper Main Street
Mountcharles, Co. Donegal
Ireland
Telephone: (011-353-73) 21672

Clothing: Aran hand-knit sweaters, vests, shawls, hats, mittens, gloves and sweater jackets for men, women and children.

A brochure with prices is available. All prices include postage and insurance. Everything is available in natural wool shades, but you can also order dyed colors. A woman's crew-neck sweater was $55.00 when we priced it and we saw an Aran sweater in the same pattern at home for $135.00.

Checks, money orders, bank drafts, MasterCard and Visa are accepted.

Kevin & Howlin, Ltd.
31 Nassau Street
Dublin 2
Ireland
Telephone: (011-353-1) 770257

Clothing: Donegal tweed jackets, suits, hats and ties; shetland, lamb's-wool and cashmere sweaters; Aran hand-knit sweaters.

Fabric: handwoven Donegal tweeds by the yard.

We received a brochure, fabric samples and a self-measuring chart. This is a comprehensive measuring chart with body types, et cetera. The seventeen magnificent swatches we received ranged from almost solids to multicolored plaids. Jackets are priced at about $175.00, including mailing and insurance.

Checks are accepted.

Kinlock Anderson & Son
45 High Street
Edinburgh EH1 1SR
Scotland
Telephone: (011-44-31) 556 6961

Clothing: Highland dress clothing for men in 350 authentic tartans; kilts, jackets, hats, sweaters, lace jabots, kilt stockings and shoes.

Ladies' clothing: skirts, knitwear, blouses, hats, scarves and evening sashes.

Tartan fabric by the meter.

Jewelry by Scottish silversmiths: kilt pins, sash brooches, etc.

If you're Scottish and a long way from home, this is where to shop when you need an authentic tartan.

We received a brochure with price list, size chart and a few fabric samples.

Checks or credit cards are accepted. Postage and insurance charges are additional.

Le Tricoteur & Co., Ltd.
Pitronnerie Road
St. Peter Port
Guernsey
Channel Islands, England
Telephone: (011-44-481) 26214
Telex: 4191578 "attention Le Tricoteur"

Guernsey sweaters: pullovers, and jacket style with zipper; hats and scarves; all items are 100 percent new, English wool.

These full-fashioned hand-finished traditional Guernsey sweaters are available in ten different colors. A small brochure is available showing the two styles and the range of colors.

Prices are given in pounds sterling and run about twenty-one pounds ($29.40) for a woman's sweater.

Airfreight to the United States is about $6.00 additional.

International postal money orders, bank drafts and credit cards are accepted.

Loden Plankl
Michaelplatz 6
1010 Vienna
Austria
Telephone: (011-43-222) 52 58 68

Clothing: typical Austrian dirndls, dresses, jackets and blouses for women and children.

Lederhosen for boys.
Wool suits for men, women and children.
Loden coats, capes, hats and jackets for men, women
and children.
Tyrolian hats for men and women.

Brochures are available. Prices are sent only for specific inquiries. Lederhosen were priced at $22.00 to $33.00 and postage was $8.00 additional.

> **Lulle Otterstad**
> **(The Sweater Lady)**
> **Solligt 2**
> **Oslo 2**
> **Norway**
> **Telephone: (011-47-2) 56 27 00**

Clothing for men, women and children in both hand and
machine knits, by Dale of Norway: sweaters, caps, mit-
tens and socks.

Two brochures with size charts and price lists are available. A wide range of designs, patterns and color combinations in 100 percent wool are available. Adult-size sweaters range from $50.00 to $75.00. Postage is an additional $5.00 per sweater. Prices are given in Norwegian kroner. Her motto is, "If you can't come to Norway, I'll send it to you."

Checks are accepted.

Robert Tailoring & Co., Ltd.
M-12 Mandarin Hotel
G.P.O. Box 3833, Hong Kong
Hong Kong
Telephone: (011-852-5) 241 348

Custom-made clothing: shirts and suits.

When "hubby" saw that we had entered J.C.'s tailor, he insisted that we enter his. Robert is a superb tailor (he made me the most beautiful raw silk blazer), but we have never really dealt with him by mail. We sent a telex to him the last time we were headed in that direction and told him what we wanted and he immediately sent us some sample swatches. Robert Tailoring is certainly worth a letter if you are looking for quality workmanship.

Royal Handknits
Strandhuse 68
Mail-Order Department
DK 5700 Svendborg
Denmark
Telephone: (011-45-9) 22 18 00

Clothing: sweaters and matching hats in Scandinavian patterns and colors, both machine knit and hand knit of North Atlantic wool.
Icelandic-type jackets and coats.

Two brochures were received in response to our request. There is an unusually large selection of interesting yoke and all-over designs. The shop has its own staff of knitters and is constantly developing new designs and color combinations. The brochures include a size comparison and measurement chart, and price list. Prices are in U.S. dollars and 22 percent Danish VAT has already been deducted. Prices include postage and insurance by surface mail. Airmail is additional.

There is a Christmas gift service, but you must order before November 10 to allow for shipping.

Personal checks, money orders and credit cards are accepted.

Salon de Mode Soong
25 Mody Road, 1st floor
Kowloon
Hong Kong
Telephone: (011-852-3) 660 480

Ladies' clothing: jackets, coats, suits, skirts, slacks, dresses, etc.

Do you have a favorite dress that doesn't quite fit any longer or perhaps looks somewhat tired and worn? This Hong Kong dressmaker will take that favorite garment and create it anew. All you have to do is specify the color and type of material you want and the shop will send sample swatches and a price list for your consideration. If you can't send a garment, you can send pictures of the styles you wish copied.

There is a complete measuring chart for you to fill in and return.

Payment may be made by check.

St. Andrews Woolen Mill
5, Pilmour Links
St. Andrews, Fife
Scotland KY16 9BR
Telephone: (011-44-334) 72366

Clothing: Kilts for women and children.
Shetland, Fair Isle, lamb's-wool, cashmere and Aran sweaters.
Scarves, tams and ties.

Blankets and lap rugs: mohair and wool, and in tartan plaids.

Yarns: shetland, Aran, acrylic, wool and nylon.
Knitting kits for Fair Isle sweaters, children's and ladies'.

Fabric: tweeds and tartans; tartans come in acrylic or 100 percent wool; fabrics to match yarns are also available.

Sheepskins in single or double size.

Descriptive literature, price lists and yarn samples are available. Prices are given in English pounds. Postage and packing are additional and are billed after the package is sent.

Yarn prices are excellent and for the novice knitter the Fair Isle kit is a bargain at approximately $17.00. The complicated, designed yoke is already hand knit and all you have to do is knit the body and sleeves and join them to the yoke. All materials and instructions are included. A full sized, 52-by-67-inch mohair and wool (70-30) blanket is approximately $33.00. A mohair blanket that we saw recently was selling for $110.00 in the United States.

This company offers an instant money refund guarantee on all merchandise. If you don't like what you get, return it and the store will send a cash refund.

Payment is accepted by check, money order or credit card.

Sweater Market
Frederiksberggade 15
DK 1459 Copenhagen
Denmark
Telephone: (011-45-1) 15 27 73

Clothing: Scandinavian wool sweaters for men and women, almost all of which are hand knit.
Hand-knit hats to match the sweaters.

A full-color brochure is available showing the range of beautiful designs. If you would prefer other color combinations than the ones shown, the shop will try to meet your requirements. If you are not completely satisfied, an exchange or a refund can be arranged.

These are some of the nicest sweaters we've seen and the prices are excellent, about one half U.S. prices. The price, in U.S. dollars, includes handling, postage and insurance. The Danish VAT has already been deducted.

Payment is accepted by check or charge card.

W. Bill, Ltd.
93 New Bond Street
London W1Y 9LA
England
Telephone: (011-44-1) 629 2837

Clothing: sweaters for men and women in lamb's wool, cashmere, Fair Isle and Aran knit.
 Ladies' wool skirts, kilts, capes and suits.
 Children's sweaters and kilts.
 Accessories: hats, gloves, socks, ties, scarves and stoles, canes/walking sticks.

Fabric by the meter.

Blankets and traveling rugs.

Color catalogs and price lists are available. If you are interested in tweeds and suitings, name the color family, and the store will send you fabric swatches.

Kilted skirts can be yours at savings of 50 to 70 percent. If this is what you want, ask for samples of authentic and modern tartans.

Prices are given in U.S. dollars. Postage, packing and insurance is a small additional fee.

Payment is accepted by check or charge card.

This company comes to the United States every year with a traveling display of its merchandise. You will be notified in advance of its arrival.

W. S. Robertson Outfitters, Ltd.
41 Bank Street
Galashiels
Scotland
Telephone: (011-44-896) 2152

Sweaters and knitwear for men and women in shetland, lamb's wool, and cashmere by Pringle of Scotland.

Knitwear catalogs with printed color charts are available. The VAT of 15 percent will be deducted from the prices, which are given in pounds sterling.

A ladies' single-weight round-neck pullover in cashmere is 77 pounds sterling, less 15 percent, plus $6.00 insured airmail, for a total of $97.63. This is about one half the cost of a Pringle cashmere sweater in the United States. A man's double-weight lamb's wool round-neck pullover is 29.50 pounds sterling, less 15 percent plus $6.00 insured airmail for a total of $41.10. Surface mail is only $3.00 per item.

Bank drafts, international money orders and checks are accepted.

William Schmidt & Co.
Karl Johans Gate 41
Oslo 1
Norway

Clothing: Scandinavian sweaters of 100 percent wool for men, women and children. Hand knits and Voss brand machine knits.

Accessories: hats, caps, gloves, mittens, scarves and slippers.

Full-color brochures are available showing styles, patterns and colors. Prices and a measuring chart are included. Deduct 16.67 percent VAT from the prices given in Danish kroner for an estimated price. The exact price in U.S. dollars is available upon request. Our estimates show a savings of about 50 percent on hand-knit items.

Payment accepted by check or bank money order.

If you have browsed through the designer boutiques at home, you may wish to write to some of the following addresses to see whether these companies accept mail orders. The addresses are for the designers' ready-to-wear and accessory boutiques.

Balenciaga
10, avenue George V
75008 Paris, France

Pierre Balmain
44, rue François 1er
75008 Paris, France

Cacharel
165, rue de Rennes
75006 Paris, France

Chanel
42, avenue Montaigne
75008 Paris, France

Chloë
60, faubourg Saint-Honoré
75008 Paris, France

Courrèges
46, faubourg Saint-Honoré
75008 Paris, France

Pierre Cardin
83, faubourg Saint-Honoré
75008 Paris, France

Louis Feraud
88, faubourg Saint-Honoré
75008 Paris, France

Givenchy
3, avenue George V
75008 Paris, France

Daniel Hechter
12, faubourg Saint-Honoré
75008 Paris, France

Lanvin
2, faubourg Saint-Honoré
75008 Paris, France

A wide range of accessories is available.

Ted Lapidus
1, place Saint-Germain-des-Prés
75006 Paris, France

Guy Larouche
29, avenue Montaigne
75008 Paris, France

Hanae Mori
17, avenue Montaigne
75008 Paris, France

Nina Ricci
39, avenue Montaigne
75008 Paris, France

A wide range of accessories, jewelry and perfumes as well as clothing is available.

Sonia Rykiel
6, rue de Grenelle
75006 Paris, France

Scarves, hats, gloves, bags as well as her famous knits are available here.

Yves Saint-Laurent
38, faubourg Saint-Honoré
75008 Paris, France

Emmanuel Ungaro
25, faubourg Saint-Honoré
75008 Paris, France

Valentino
19, avenue Montaigne
75008 Paris, France

For more clothing, *see*

Brown Thomas & Co.
Cash & Co., Ltd.
China Products Co. (H.K.), Ltd.

Chung Kiu Chinese Prod. Emporium
Den Permanente A/S
Emerald
F. Rubbrecht
Fallers, Ltd.
Galeries Lafayette
Harrods
Hermes
Husfliden of Bergen
Illum
Schilz
Schneider Riding Boot Co., Ltd.
Shannon Mail Order
St. Patrick's Down
Tartan Gift Shop
Tiroler Heimatwerk
Yue Hwa Chinese Prod. Emporium

Cookware and
Kitchenware

Fʀᴏᴍ ᴡᴏᴏᴅᴇɴ sᴘᴏᴏɴs ᴛᴏ copper pots, from knives for left-handers to mandolins, these are the places from which you can outfit a kitchen or find that one special tool you need.

—————————————————————

—————————————————————

Coutellerie du Mont-Blanc
7, rue du Mont-Blanc
Case Postale 212
CH-1211 Geneva
Switzerland
Telephone: (011-41-22) 32 39 69

Victorinox Swiss Army knives and pocket knives.
  Professional knives for butchers, cooks, etc.
  Custom-made knives for the collector.
  Scissors.
  Christofle silver flatware.
  Pewter items.

A brochure on the Swiss Army knives is available. Prices are given in Swiss francs and do not include postage. Mailing and insurance for one army knife is approximately 7 Swiss francs (about $3.25). Prices on Swiss Army knives are about 50 percent of U.S. list prices. The model "Grand Prix" lists for $39.95 and is available from this company for 40.4 Swiss francs (approximately $20.00).

They are very nice people to deal with and when we requested an item which the store did not carry, they went so far as to offer to find it for us in a neighboring shop, if we would give them some additional information. If you want something other than a Swiss Army knife, be specific in your request, as the store does not have a general catalog.

We have ordered two Swiss Army knives and, both times, postage and insurance were the only charges we had to add to the price.

Checks and credit cards are accepted.

E. Dehillerin
18, rue Coquillière
75001 Paris
France
Telephone: (011-33-14) 4236 5313

Cookware: a complete line of professional cooking, baking, candy-making and serving equipment.
Tin-lined copperware.
Molds for ice cream, chocolate, aspics, terrines, charlottes, cookies, etc.
Knives, meat saws, cleavers.
Wooden pepper mills of all sizes.

A catalog showing the incredible array of kitchen equipment which the store carries is available. This is a store for the serious cook. It has been supplying equipment to French chefs for the last 165 years. All those hard-to-find items that you can't find elsewhere are commonplace here.

Send your list after you have browsed through the catalog and the store will send you prices, with shipping, according to the prevailing exchange rate.

Checks are accepted.

J. A. Henckels Zwillingswerk AG
Weinstrasse 12
8000 Munich
Germany
Telephone: (011-49-89) 22 21 35

Henckel knives and knife sets for cooks.
  Carving sets, cleavers, poultry shears.
  Sharpening steels for home and professional use.
  Professional knife sets in fitted carrying cases.
  Professional butcher knives.
  Kitchen tool sets: spatulas, ladles, potato mashers, whips, bottle openers and spoons.

A complete line of scissors, some for the left-handed.

Manicuring tools and gift sets.

Catalogs without price lists are available. Prices, including shipping, are quoted according to your choices and the prevailing rate of exchange.

One item that tickled our fancy was a grooming kit for a beard or mustache. It contained a small combination comb/brush, trimming scissors and a mirror in a leather carrying case. We thought that this would make a great gift.

Checks are accepted.

For more cookware and kitchenware, *see*

Anything Left Handed, Ltd.
Arabia Rorstrand Center
Bi-Rite Photo & Electronics
Den Permanente A/S
Illum
Illums Bolighus
OY Stockmann AB
Peter
Rosenthal Studio-Haus
Scandinavian Center

Crystal

Iᶠ ᴄʀʏꜱᴛᴀʟ ꜱᴇᴛꜱ ʏᴏᴜʀ ᴇʏᴇꜱ sparkling—but they glaze over at the prices—you can very often get three pieces of stemware by mail for the price of one piece in the store.

A B Nordiska Kompaniet
S-103 74 Stockholm
Sweden
Telephone: (011-46-8) 762 8000
Telex: 103 57 enco s

Crystal: Orrefors, Kosta Boda and other Scandinavian brands of stemware, tableware and giftware.

China, ceramics and cookware: Scandinavian brands.

Flatware and hollow ware in silver, stainless and pewter.

This is a large department store. Brochures are available in many different categories. A detailed cost estimate, shipping included, with the VAT already deducted, will be sent.

Checks and credit cards are accepted. However,

there is an additional $3.00 charge if you use a check in U.S. dollars.

A. B. Schou
4 NY Ostergade
1101 Copenhagen K
Denmark
Telephone: (011-45-1) 13 80 95

Crystal stemware and tableware: iittala, Orrefors, Hadelands, Holmegaard, Kosta Boda, Marcolin, Atlantis, Goebel, Lalique, Nachtmann, Oberursel, Riedel, Swarovski, Waterford, etc.

China dinnerware: Bing & Grondahl, Porsgrund, Royal Copenhagen, Royal Worcester, Spode, Villeroy & Boch, etc.

Figurines: Bing & Grondahl, Royal Copenhagen, Goebel, Herend, Hummel, Lalique, Lladro, Nao, Royal Worcester, Swarovski, etc.

Giftware by Bing & Grondahl, iittala, Herend, Lalique, Orrefors, Royal Copenhagen, Royal Worcester, Waterford.

Collectibles: plates, cups, mugs and bells by Bing & Grondahl, Porsgrund, Royal Copenhagen and Royal Doulton.
   Dolls by Bing & Grondahl.
   Crystal sculptures by Mats Jonasson.

Christmas items: Spode "Christmas Tree" china, Porsgrund "Hearts and Pines" china and Marcolin handmade crystal Christmas trees; crystal tree ornaments.

Many brochures are available as well as two catalogs. The porcelain catalog is $4.00 and the crystal catalog is $2.00. These charges will be deducted from your first order, except for orders of collector's items such as Christmas plates.

Prices are given in U.S. dollars and include postage and insurance. The Orrefors "Classic Decanter" is $122.00 delivered, compared with $210.00 locally. However, our spot check of Waterford prices revealed negligible savings. So check prices on non-Scandinavian items before you order.

Payment is accepted by check or money order.

Art et Sélection, s.p.r.l.
83, Marché aux Herbes
1000 Brussels
Belgium
Telephone: (011-32-2) 511 8448

Crystal stemware and barware: Val St. Lambert, Atlantis, Baccarat, Daum, Lalique, St. Louis and Waterford.

China dinnerware by Bernardaud, Coquet, Haviland and Hutschenreuther.

Silver flatware and hollow ware by Christofle and Ercuis.

Giftware: Val St. Lambert vases, bowls, candlesticks, ashtrays, etched occasional pieces and paperweights.

Figurines and crystal sculptures by Val St. Lambert and Lalique.

A catalog which shows the selection of clear and colored crystal is available. Prices in Belgian francs, minus the Belgian VAT, were sent on requested items. Our comparisons of Val St. Lambert stemware, which is relatively hard to come by, show that the prices are excellent. Savings are about 50 percent.

Checks or American Express cards are accepted, and they even included an AmEx form for our convenience.

If you're ever in the neighborhood of the Grand' Place, this store is a crystal wonderland; but don't forget, the prices in the store include the VAT and you may have to spend a given minimum before the VAT is deducted. Ask.

Baccarat
30 bis, rue de Paradis
75010 Paris
France
Telephone: (011-33-1) 4770 6430
Telex: BACCRIS 290947 F

Crystal stemware and barware by Baccarat.

Giftware: vases, candlesticks, hurricane lamps, bowls, ashtrays, covered containers, ice buckets, decanters, saltcellars and obelisks.

Figurines: clear, frosted and black glass animals.

All merchandise is Baccarat. There are several brochures available. Prices are only given on items for which you specifically ask. As we have shopped in this store in person we know that the savings are approximately 50 percent. The *lapin* (rabbit) figurine was $26.00 in Paris compared to $55.00 at home. Personal checks are accepted. Credit cards are not accepted on mail orders.

C. J. Josephssons Glas & Porslin AB
Korsgatan 12
Box 339
401-25 Göteborg
Sweden
Telephone: (011-46-31) 17 56 15

Orrefors and Kosta Boda crystal.

China tableware and giftware.

Catalogs are available and will be sent on the specific brand of your choice. Nineteen percent is deducted from the price for the Swedish VAT. Eight percent is added for insurance and packing. Freight or mailing charges are by weight of the parcel.
    Checks are accepted.

Cristal Lalique
11, rue Royale
75008 Paris
France
Telephone: (011-33-1) 265 3370
Telex: 641653 F

Crystal stemware by Lalique.

Figurines in Lalique crystal.

Crystal giftware by Lalique: vases, decanters, coasters, ice buckets, candy dishes and covered bowls, perfume atomizers and bottles, ring holders, caviar servers and lamp bases.

All items are by Lalique. However, because of commercial agreements, orders cannot be accepted unless you have previously been in the Paris store. Lucky us! One of our children has shopped there in person.

For those of you who have not yet been to Paris, check our other crystal, gift and figurine listings for Lalique.

Hamilton & Inches, Ltd.
87 George Street
Edinburgh EH2 3EY
Scotland
Telephone: (011-44-31) 225 4899

Edinburgh of Scotland crystal stemware.

Jewelry: kilt pins and clan brooches.
  Watches and clocks.

Giftware: silver and Edinburgh crystal.

Hamilton & Inches does not have a general catalog but is more than happy to send individual brochures and price lists, with the VAT still included. The white wine or tall champagne glass is each 17.50 pounds sterling ($24.50), compared to $60.00 in New York for the "Star of Edinburgh" pattern. Sherry glasses are 13.95 pounds each ($19.53), compared to $48.00, and the cost of sending six of these is about 10.00 pounds sterling.

In case you're interested in the "Thistle" pattern, it is currently selling locally for $95.00 a water glass

and $75.00 a champagne flute or red wine glass.
  Postage, packing and insurance charges depend
upon the weight of the parcel.

Holmegaards Glassworks, Ltd.
15 Oestergade
DK 1100 Copenhagen K
Denmark
Telephone: (011-45-3) 74 62 00
Telex: 46275

Holmegaard hand-blown and handmade crystal stem-
ware and barware.

Giftware by Holmegaard: vases, bowls, candlesticks,
carafes and pitchers.
  Hand-blown Victorian-style glass oil lamps.
  Art glass bowls and vases.

A giftware catalog is available. Prices are sent after
you make your selection and will include postage,
packing and insurance, with Danish VAT deducted.
  Checks are accepted.

Lobmeyr
Karntnerstrasse 26
A 1015 Vienna
Austria
Telephone: (011-43-222) 52 21 89
Telex: 1 35139 glas a

Crystal stemware and barware.

Crystal chandeliers and lighting fixtures.

China dinnerware: Herend and other brands.

Giftware: crystal vases, bowls, candlesticks, covered candy dishes, etc.
   Herend china serving pieces and gift items, large and small.

A catalog and complete price lists are available for Lobmeyr crystal. This magnificent crystal has been produced for over 150 years. A variety of hand-blown crystal is produced. It is then cut, etched or engraved depending upon the pattern.
   This is the firm that produced the chandeliers for the Metropolitan Opera House in New York City and the Vienna State Opera House.
   Prices are given in Austrian shillings; 20 percent VAT will be deducted.
   Checks are accepted.

Rasper & Sohne
Waagplatz 1
5020 Salzburg
Austria
Telephone: (011-43-662) 41 6 73

Crystal: Lobmeyr stemware, Riedel glass and crystal, Swarovski crystal, etc.

Giftware in crystal and porcelain: Swarovski animals, candlesticks, table ornaments, etc.

Collectibles: Swarovski crystal animals.

Specific brochures are available but there is no general catalog. In response to our inquiry we received the

Swarovski boutique catalog and price list in Austrian schillings. This brochure shows the silver crystal animals, candleholders, covered containers, paperweights, bowls, vases, et cetera.

The large owl is priced at 820 Austrian schillings, about $47.00 at this time. Locally, it sells for $85.00 plus tax. Shipping and insurance charges will be calculated after you have made your selection.

Your personal check will be accepted.

Silverbergs
Baltzarsgatan 31
Box 4051
203 11 Malmö 4
Sweden
Telephone: (011-46-40) 740 80
Telex: 324 78 DETE S.

The complete Orrefors line of crystal stemware and barware.

Giftware: Orrefors crystal vases, bowls, decanters, candlesticks, crystal tree ornaments, perfume bottles, etc.

Orrefors crystal figurines.

Some places are a pleasure to deal with, and this is one of those places! There were no brochures to send in response to our inquiry about Orrefors crystal, so we received the store copy of the catalog showing the entire Orrefors line. This book was airmailed to us with a request to take our time and look through it, show it to our friends, et cetera, and when we were finished shopping, to please return it. This is not normally sent out of the store. We returned the catalog by airmail along with a request for prices on the "Illusion" and "Harmony" patterns, as the catalog had no prices. The response was quick and the prices are excellent. The prices are given in Swedish kroner and 19 percent VAT is deducted.

Packing, shipping and insurance are determined by weight. The price of mailing twelve to twenty-four glasses was 132 Sw.K., or about $20.00.

The savings averaged 60 to 70 percent depending upon the size of the glass.

One note: In the Orrefors catalog the pattern we know as "Harmony" was called "Blanche," so if you have a picture of the pattern that you want, send it with your inquiry.

Checks are accepted.

Switzer & Company
Grafton Street
P.O. Box 132
Dublin 2
Ireland

Waterford crystal stemware and barware.

Waterford chandeliers and lighting fixtures.

Giftware: Waterford vases, bowls, centerpieces, sugars and creamers, saltcellars, candlesticks, ashtrays, celery and bonbon dishes, decanters, cutlery with Waterford handles, perfume bottles, etc.

Switzer is another of our favorite places. As we get a great deal of mail from overseas, it took us awhile to figure out what store had sent us brochures and price lists in a plain brown unmarked envelope. Our only clue was the postmark. By the process of elimination we were able to figure out it was Switzer. This took some doing, but it was well worth the effort as these are the best prices that we have seen for Waterford crystal.

Our latest purchase was a celery dish at $47.00, including postage and insurance. This dish sells for $101.00 plus tax in the United States. The crystal-handled cake server runs about $27.00 at Switzer, instead of $69.50, and the salad server set is about $49.50, instead of $150.00 at home.

For those of you interested in stemware, we did a price comparison of the water goblets. The "Sheila" pattern, which sells for $33.00 here, is 13.09 Irish pounds ($17.25). "Alana" is $45.00 here and is 21.30 Irish pounds ($26.65). "Lismore" is $33.50 here and 20.16 Irish pounds ($25.25). "Colleen" is $41.50 here and 22.66 Irish pounds ($28.30). The percentage saved varies with the pattern you choose, but with these kinds of savings available we have been able to give some lovely wedding, anniversary and Christmas gifts. We are able to treat ourselves as well.

Prices are given in Irish pounds with the VAT already deducted.

Checks, money orders and credit cards are accepted.

NOTE: Cash & Co., Ltd., is the mail-order arm of the Switzer Group of stores and sometimes Switzer will answer your inquiry by sending you Cash's catalog. The catalog has been showing more and more Waterford items, so this may be the way Switzer will respond in the future.

For more crystal, *see*

A. H. Riise Gift Shops
Arabia Rorstrand Center
Brown Thomas & Co.
Cambet
Cash & Co., Ltd.
Chinacraft of London, Ltd.
Christofle
Den Permanente A/S
E. Bakalowits Sohne GMBH
Editions Paradis
Emerald
The English Shop
Fallers, Ltd.
Focke & Meltzer
Galeries Lafayette
The General Trading Co.
Harrods
Illum
Illums Bolighus
Little Switzerland
Magasin
OY Stockmann AB
Reject China Shops
Rosenthal Studio-Haus
Scandinavian Center
Shannon Mail Order
Standing Decors 2
Tartan Gift Shop
Thomas Goode & Co., Ltd.
Zoellner-Rosenthal

Department Stores

Y OU CAN USUALLY FIND
everything you want under one roof in a department
store. Ask for what you want; the store probably has
it, even if we haven't listed it. We have also included
in this chapter those mail-order catalog firms that
have a variety of merchandise similar to that of a
department store.

Brown Thomas & Company
15 Grafton Street
Dublin 2
Ireland
Telephone: (011-353-1) 77 68 61
Telex: 24495

Crystal stemware and giftware: Waterford, Cavan, Tyrone, etc.
Crystal lighting fixtures by Waterford.

China dinnerware: Belleek, Wedgwood, Coalport, Royal Albert, Royal Doulton, Aynsley and Royal Worcester.

Figurines and florals by Coalport and others.

Linens and lace: tablecloths, placemats and napkins in double-damask Irish linen, hand-embroidered Irish linen and hand-worked Madeira.

Linen tea towels and handkerchiefs.

Hand-crocheted lace "bowls," table squares, coasters, etc.

Classic Irish bed linen by Lamont.

Clothing: women's Irish tweed coats, capes and suits; kilted skirts; Irish crochet suits and dresses; Aran sweaters for men, women and children; men's Irish tweed jackets, ties and caps; men's doeskin vests and cashmere sweaters; Burberrys raincoats.

Blankets: goose- and duck-down quilts, pure wool Foxford tartan rugs (blankets).

Handwoven bedspreads in natural Aran wool.

Fabric: plain or Donegal plaid mohair by the yard, handwoven tweed fabric.

Handwoven tweed-skirt packs for the do-it-yourselfer.

Celtic jewelry in silver, gold and enamel.

This is a department store with an export catalog that presents a sampling of the varied merchandise it carries. The price list was out of print when we wrote, so a second letter was required for prices and postal information. All orders are acknowledged by an airmail postcard. This is where we bought Waterford crystal stemware many years ago. In fact, this is what started us off on our quest for the best for less.

Personal checks and credit cards are accepted.

Cash & Company, Ltd.
P.O. Box 47, St. Patrick's Street
Cork
Ireland
Telephone: 1-800-972-1000

China dinnerware: Belleek, Aynsley, Burleigh, Coalport, Denby, Johnson Brothers, Mason, Portmeirion, Royal Doulton, Royal Worcester, Spode, Villeroy & Boch and Wedgwood.

Children's sets: Royal Doulton's "Bunnykins," Royal Worcester's "Cabbage Patch" and Wedgwood's "Peter Rabbit."

Waterford crystal stemware and barware.

Crystal lighting fixtures, cutlery and pendants by Waterford.

Figurines of china, crystal, wood and metal: Anri, Aynsley, Border Fine Arts, Capodimonte, Goebel, Irish Dresden, Lladro, Royal Doulton, Royal Doulton Beswick, Royal Worcester.

Giftware: china and crystal items (see brands listed above); domed and carriage clocks, barometers, chess sets, pewter mugs and punch-bowl sets, banks, children's and dolls' dishes, heraldic shields, stuffed animals and dolls, dresser sets, wall plaques, pocket knives, nautical plaques and gift items, bookends, brass door knockers, porcelain liquor labels, golfing aids and accessories, walking sticks, etc.

Pipes by Oppenheimer.

Collectibles: paperweights, Bossons' heads, Toby mugs, Nisbet dolls, miniature tea services, Beatrix Potter figu-

*rines, collectors' plates, thimbles, Coalport "cottages,"
Wade porcelain "villages," cups and saucers, figurines
(see list above), etc., etc., etc.*

*Clothing: hand-knit and machine-knit vests, sweaters,
hats and scarves in wool, cashmere and lamb's wool,
including Aran knitware of all kinds.*
  Kilted skirts for children and women.
  *Donegal tweed jackets, assorted caps and scarves in
tweeds and plaids.*
  Shawls, Celtic cloaks, ponchos, capes.
  Nottingham lace blouses, dresses and children's dresses.
  Sheepskin slippers.
  Kinsale smocks.
  Etc., etc., etc.

*Christmas and religious items: crèche sets; figurines by
Anri, Hummel, Goebel, Royal Doulton, Lladro, Irish
Dresden, etc.*
  Christmas spoons and plates.
  Tree ornaments in wood, glass and china.
  Christmas china: Spode's "Christmas Tree" and Mason's "Christmas Village" patterns.
  Celtic crosses.

Food: Irish smoked salmon, Mrs. Beeton's Plum Pudding and Gordon's English mustard sets.

Irish linen: tablecloths, placemats, napkins, handkerchiefs and knitware.

*Books: Beatrix Potter stories; books about Ireland. Books
about collectibles: Bossons, Waterford, Wedgwood and
Lladro.*
  The Book of Kells *reproduction.*

Once you've requested a catalog from Cash's you will likely find one in your mailbox several times a year. On occasion there are even sales brochures. This is a good general catalog with a large variety of merchandise that changes with the seasons. Note the toll-free phone number for credit card orders only. Prices are quoted in U.S. dollars. Packing, mailing and insurance charges are additional. Average delivery time is four weeks and you have thirty days in which to return unsatisfactory merchandise.

We have ordered a number of times from this catalog and have been most satisfied. The one time that we needed to make a return, the store gave us a credit equal to our return postage costs.

A hand-knit Aran sweater with dolman sleeves was priced at $110.00 and looked very much like a sweater advertised by a New York shop for over $200.00.

Wedgwood's "Runnymede" pattern lists for $195.00 for one five-piece place setting. We saw it on sale locally for $156.00. Cash's price is $107.00 per five-piece place setting.

Our price comparison on the new Waterford cutlery showed a great savings. For instance, the salad set is $66.00 in the catalog instead of $150.00 here. The cake server is priced at $36.00 instead of $69.50.

If the piece of Waterford you want is not in the catalog, there is a special address and phone number you can use for additional information.

Checks and credit cards are accepted.

China Products Co. (H.K.), Ltd.
Lok Sing Centre
Yee Wo Street
Hong Kong
Hong Kong
Telephone: (011-852-5) 798 321
Telex: 61308 CPCLD HX

Porcelain and ceramics: Oriental tea services and dinnerware; Western-style dinnerware in Oriental patterns; vases, lamp bases, garden stools, figurines and flower pots.
Ceramic objets d'art.

Figurines: porcelain carvings from Shiwan, woven bamboo animals, cork, wood, soapstone, bone, jade and ivory carvings, and lacquer figurines from Foochow.

Giftware: rattan, straw and bamboo articles; ink stones, ink sticks, calligraphy brushes, porcelain containers with red "chop" inks; small chess sets, dolls, doll furniture and miniatures; kites, embroidery, wall hangings, etc., etc.
Cloisonné vases, display plates, bowls, temple and ginger jars, boxes, ashtrays, napkin rings, beads and pendants, salt and pepper sets and smoking sets.
Lacquerware trays, coffee and tea sets, vases, boxes, bowls, multicompartmented serving dishes.
Small, stuffed satin items such as fish and animals (some with loops for hanging).

Collectibles: Snuff bottles made of semiprecious materials, glass, cloisonné, horn and lacquer.
Jade and ivory carvings.
Cinnabar bowls, vases and display plates.

Cloisonné vases, bowls, covered ginger and temple jars, display plates and miniatures.

Oriental rugs.

Rosewood and camphorwood furniture.

Oriental screens: lacquer, inlaid, Corramandel and silk.

Food: an extensive assortment of Chinese teas.

Clothing: silk mandarin coats, dressing gowns and pajamas; embroidered, beaded and petit-point evening bags.

Silk fabric by the yard.

Jewelry: Cloisonné, cinnabar and semiprecious-stone bead necklaces and pendants; enameled jewelry.

Chinese musical instruments.

China Products is a large department store with two branches. It deals exclusively with merchandise made in the People's Republic of China.

This mail-order catalog comes in four packages containing colored, numbered photographs with descriptions on the reverse side. A separate price list in Hong Kong dollars was sent for the cloisonné items we inquired about. We found that the prices were less than 75 percent of U.S. prices. We think that the small, stuffed satin items we mentioned in giftware would make wonderful Christmas tree ornaments.

The overseas service department will take care of mailing or shipping the merchandise.

Checks are accepted.

Chinese Arts & Crafts, Ltd.
233-239 Nathan Road, 1-3/F
Kowloon
Hong Kong
Telephone: (011-852-3) 670 061
Telex: 64199 CACHK HX

Giftware: cloisonné and cinnabar vases, bowls, covered ginger and temple jars, display plates and jewelry, as well as cloisonné miniatures; bamboo and straw items, silk flowers, Peking glass flowers and trees, brass animals, wall hangings, small, stuffed satin figures (some with loops for hanging).

Porcelain and ceramics: vases, bowls, tea sets, dinnerware, etc.

Figurines: soapstone, horn, jade, ivory, wood, porcelain and ceramic.

Oriental rugs.

Rosewood and lacquer furniture.
  Oriental screens: silk and lacquer.

Silk fabrics by the yard.

Linens: embroidered and appliquéd tablecloths, placemats, napkins, runners, bread-basket liners and guest towels.

Clothing: silk mandarin jackets, dressing gowns and blouses.
  Embroidered, beaded and petit-point evening bags.

This large department store has four branches in Hong Kong, all filled with Chinese-made merchandise; and I've personally shopped in each and every one (but they've surely restocked by now!). The prices are very good but remember—and this applies to all Hong Kong stores—shipping can be expensive on heavy items like furniture.

Unfortunately, the store was out of catalogs when we wrote, but the response was very prompt, so do write.

When we wrote we inquired about a ten-inch cloisonné vase. We received a photograph of two vases with different designs and a letter giving the prices in HK dollars, the mailing costs and even the current exchange rate. A ten-inch vase on a lacquered wood stand is HK$330.00, and sea mail is HK$90.00 additional. The complete cost is $53.25 in the United States. If you tried to buy this at home it would cost in the neighborhood of $300.00.

Sets of six hand-embroidered birds, animals or clowns ranged from $4.50 to $5.50 a set. These would make great Christmas tree decorations and you could easily add loops for hanging to any that do not already have them.

Payment is accepted by bank draft in Hong Kong dollars.

Chung Kiu Chinese Prod. Emporium
Arts & Crafts Branch
528-532 Nathan Road
Kowloon
Hong Kong
Telephone: (011-852-3) 023 515

Porcelain and ceramics: tea sets, Chinese dinner services, Western dinner services with Oriental designs, display plates, miniature tea sets, vases, garden seats, etc.

Figurines: porcelain, ceramic, wood, bone, ivory, jade, turquoise, agate, tiger-eye, malachite and cloisonné.

Giftware: chess sets, fans, straw, bamboo and rattan items; rosewood jewlery and cigarette boxes, Peking glass flowers in pots, Peking glass fruits and figurines, small stuffed satin ornaments with loops for hanging; dolls, Chinese paper cuts, ink stones, calligraphy brushes, wall hangings, etc.

Cloisonné and cinnabar vases, bowls, display plates, covered ginger and temple jars, ashtrays, napkin rings, boxes, smoking sets, seasoning sets, jewelry and figurines.

Lacquerware trays, coffee, tea and wine sets, writing sets, salad sets, boxes, napkin rings, smoking sets, etc.

Collectibles: snuff bottles, antique porcelains, carvings in jade, ivory, etc.; cloisonné and cinnabar items.

Clothing: silk dressing gowns, pajamas and nightgowns, scarves, men's silk shirts, etc.

Embroidered, beaded and petit-point evening bags.

Linens: cutwork, embroidered, appliquéd and Venetian lace tablecloths, luncheon sets, runners, placemats and napkins.

Handkerchiefs.

Jewelry: earrings, rings, bracelets, pendants, etc., in silver, gold and enamel on silver. Semiprecious-stone bead necklaces.

Silk fabrics by the yard.

Oriental rugs.

A general catalog is available but you must write for prices on specific items. What we've said about the other Chinese department stores applies here, too. All are chock-full of goodies made in mainland China.
   Checks are accepted.

Den Permanente A/S
Vesterbrogade 8
DK 1620 Copenhagen V
Denmark
Telephone: (011-45-1) 12 44 88

Sterling silver and gold jewelry in modern designs, amber bead necklaces, wood jewelry, ceramic pendants, etc.

Flatware and hollow ware by Georg Jensen, Dansk, Gense, etc.

China and ceramics: Royal Copenhagen, Dansk, Torsten Mosumgaard, Sebastian, Ole Aarsdal, Eigil Hinrichsen, Fulby Keramik, Helle Allpass, Birkerod Keramik, Nymolle, etc.

Crystal and hand-blown glass: Holmegaard, Arreso Glashytte, Ostersohytten, Snogbaek Glashytte, Jesper Kerrn-Jespersen, Snoldelev Glasbrug and Glasmagerne.

Giftware: Georg Jensen and Bent Christensen barometers, thermometers, chronometers and hygrometers; Henrik Vensild handmade knives for the sportsman; ceramic animal and troll figures, wall hangings for children's rooms, silk-screened prints, paper pendants and mobiles; ceramic, crystal and glass vases.

Christmas items: crèche with figures, Christmas tree ornaments, Santa mobile and Christmas tree wall hangings.

Toys: wooden board games and puzzles, painted wood building blocks, wood soldiers and animals, model ships.

Cookware and kitchenware: Stelton of Denmark lines of stainless and plastics; salad bowls, fondue sets, salt and pepper shakers, thermos pitchers, ice buckets, lazy Susans, broiling and serving trays.

  PP-linie line of tableware: salt and pepper mills, etc. Wooden bowls, coasters and salt and pepper mills.

Tableware in maple: cutting boards, dishes, candlesticks, napkin rings, cheese boards, salad and fruit bowls, egg cups, etc.

Linens: tablecloths, aprons, kitchen towels, tea cosies, napkins, calendars and pot holders.

Lighting fixtures and lamps.
Danish furniture, rugs and carpets.

Ladies' clothing.

This is a large department store specializing in Danish arts and crafts. It even has an interior design service if that's what you need. If you are ordering furniture, a 25 percent deposit is required.

A general catalog with a price list is available. If you have a specific request there are additional brochures.

You deduct 18 percent VAT from the prices, which are given in Danish kroner. Packing, shipping and insurance are additional.

Checks and credit cards are accepted.

Emerald
Ballingeary
County Cork
Ireland
Telex: 75378 EMOL EI

China: Belleek, Royal Tara, Adams, Aynsley, Coalport,
Royal Doulton, Royal Worcester, Spode and Wedgwood.
 China for children: Royal Doulton's "Brambly Hedge"
and "Bunnykins" sets, Wedgwood's "Peter Rabbit."

Crystal stemware, barware, giftware and lighting fix-
tures: Cavan, Galway, Tyrone and Waterford.

Figurines: Irish Dresden, Belleek, Border Fine Arts,
Lladro, Nao by Lladro, Beswick, Royal Doulton, Coal-
port, Aynsley, Anri, Hummel, Goebel and Bruno Merli.

Giftware: paperweights, stuffed animals, china tea sets,
Wedgwood Jasperware, Belleek vases, candy dishes, etc.
 Coalport and Crown Staffordshire "motto" boxes; china
mugs, ring dishes, covered boxes and floral jewelry; he-
raldic items; dresser sets, chess sets and bridge card
sets; pill boxes, china and pewter tankards, perfume
atomizers.
 Gift packs of preserves.

Collectibles: Toby jugs, Bossons' heads (masks), thim-
bles, cups and saucers, Belleek, Royal Doulton and
Wedgwood Christmas plates, Wedgwood birthday plates,
Wade "Villages," Lilliput Lane "Cottages." Irish char-
acter dolls.
 Also see Figurines listed above.

Irish linen tablecloths and napkins.

Blankets and lap rugs in tartan plaids.

Clothing: Aran wool sweaters.

Christmas and religious: rosary beads in Connemara marble and Irish bogwood; Irish Dresden Christmas tree ornaments and angel figurines; Spode "Christmas Tree" pattern china, giftware and tree ornaments; Mason's "Christmas Village" pattern china giftware, Doulton "Santa" Toby jug, Santa figurines and Christmas stockings, Hummel and Goebel angels and Goebel mangers with figurines, Royal Doulton and Wedgwood Christmas plates.

Emerald is a direct-mail catalog and once you are on the list, catalogs will arrive several times a year, including a special Christmas catalog. Prices are given in U.S. dollars and mailing and insurance charges are additional. The cost for a $50.00 order is $6.00, but the cost for a $1,000.00 order is only $28.00. This makes it very economical to do all of your shopping in one place. Any gifts can be shipped directly to the recipients, including a gift card with your message.

The Spode "Christmas Tree" pattern ornament is $9.00 in the catalog; it was $19.95 locally. We saw a three-piece "Christmas Tree" buffet service (dinner plate, cup and saucer) on sale locally for $36.80 (regularly $46.00), but the whole *five*-piece place setting was only $39.00 by mail.

Payment by check, money order or credit card is accepted.

Fallers, Ltd.
Galway
Ireland
Telephone: (011-353-91) 61226

China dinnerware: Belleek, Aynsley, Coalport, Mason, Minton, Royal Albert, Royal Doulton, Royal Worcester, Spode and Wedgwood.

China and giftware for children: "Peter Rabbit" by Wedgwood, "Bunnykins" by Royal Doulton and "Paddington" by Coalport.

Crystal stemware, barware and giftware by Cavan, Galway, Tyrone and Waterford.

Figurines: Irish Dresden, Pucane (wood figures), Belleek, Lladro, Goebel, Hummel, Royal Doulton, Capo Di Monte, Border Fine Arts, Beswick and Anri (wood).

Giftware: music boxes, Royal Tara china candlesticks and china shoes, framed flower pictures, Belleck china-handled cutlery, Wedgwood Jasperware pieces, including a new christening spoon in pink or blue; Kerry glass paperweights, Coalport and Royal Doulton wall plaques, framed prints of Ireland; brass door knockers, clocks, china "cottages," Pucane woodcuts and Caithness glass paperweights, perfume bottles and ring stands.

Dolls' china tea sets by Wedgwood.

Handwrought Irish pewter.

Personalized crystal by Clarenbridge: tankards, plates, decanter sets, desk sets and accessories.

Pipes by Peterson.

Collectibles: Bossons' heads, Belleek thimbles, Royal Doulton Toby jugs and figurines, Christmas plates by

Belleek and Wedgwood, "Villages" by Wade, "Cottages" by Lilliput Lane and Coalport, Hummel spoons and figurines.

Lladro lamps.

Also see Figurines listed above.

Christmas and religious: nativity sets by Lladro, Goebel and Pucane Crafts; Mason's "Christmas Village" china, Royal Tara's "Christmas Holly" accessory pieces, and Spode's "Christmas Tree" pattern china dinnerware and accessories; Christmas figurines and candleholders by Royal Doulton, Goebel, and Hummel; Santa Toby jug by Royal Doulton, tree ornaments by Goebel.

Royal Doulton figurine of Pope John Paul II.

Bone china "Christmas Rose" by Royal Worcester.

Books: Beatrix Potter's storybooks.

Wool blankets and lap rugs by Foxford of Ireland in traditional tartan plaids.

Linens and lace: Irish linen tablecloths, napkins, runners, and handkerchiefs; Nottingham cotton lace tablecovers.

Traditional Irish jewelry: rings, pendants, pins and charms in sterling silver and gold; Wedgwood Jasperware pendants, brooches and cufflinks, also "Peter Rabbit" china pendants.

Porcelain dolls in traditional Irish costumes.

Smoked Irish salmon from Galway Bay.

Clothing: Aran hand-knit sweaters, Aran wool sweater kits for the do-it-yourselfer, wool capes and jackets; mohair shawls, caps and scarves; men's tweed and tartan caps.

Fallers has been in business for 106 years. The catalog, which comes twice a year, contains merchandise from Ireland and other European countries. With the exception of crystal stemware and open-stock dinnerware, all prices include shipping and insurance.

A 5-inch Waterford butter dish is $29.75 (including mailing). It is $45.00 plus tax locally.

The 8-inch Lladro "Wedding" (the bride and groom) is $82.00 from Fallers and is selling for $125.00 locally.

All prices are given in U.S. dollars. Payment by check, money order or credit card is accepted.

Galeries Lafayette
40, boulevard Haussmann
Att.: Mail-Order Department
75009 Paris
France
Telephone: (011-33-1) 4282 3456
Telex: 280 357 GALFA PARIS

China dinnerware: Bernardaud, Limoges, Ceralene, Sèvres, and other European brands.

Crystal stemware and barware: Baccarat, Daum, St. Louis, Sèvres, etc.

Giftware: a large variety of crystal and china giftware.

Figurines: Baccarat, Daum and Sèvres animals.

Perfumes and toiletries for men and women.

Yarns: Anny Blatt, Chat Botté, Pingouin, etc.

This is one of the largest department stores in Paris. Like most department stores it has a huge selection of merchandise but it does not have a storewide catalog. The items listed above are easy to send for because you can identify them by manufacturer and pattern or scent name. If you are looking for a French-made product, it pays to ask here. Small folders or brochures from individual manufacturers may be available. We asked about Bernardaud china and received a few flyers.

We purchased Anny Blatt yarn at approximately $1.50 a ball instead of $3.60 for the same yarn here.

The store will deduct the VAT and then add packing and postage charges.

Checks are accepted.

Harrods
Brompton Road
London SW1X 7XL
England
Telephone: (011-44-1) 730 1234
Telex: 24319

China dinnerware: Aynsley, Coalport, Denby, Johnson Brothers, Mason, Royal Doulton, Royal Worcester, Spode, Wedgwood, Haviland, Portmeirion, Villeroy & Boch, etc., etc., etc.

Children's china: Royal Doulton's "Bunnykins," Coalport's "Paddington Bear," Wedgwood's "Peter Rabbit," etc.

Crystal stemware and barware: Metropolitan of England, Royal Brierley, Stuart, Tudor, Atlantis, Bac-

carat, Orrefors, St. Louis, Val St. Lambert, Waterford, etc.

Silver-plate flatware by George Butler of Sheffield and others.

Figurines: Baccarat, Daum and Swarovski crystal animals; Royal Worcester's "Women in Vogue"; Royal Doulton and Coalport "ladies"; porcelain dogs by Augarten of Vienna and English birds by Royal Worcester; Beswick animals, etc.

Giftware: Wedgwood Jasperware, Royal Doulton Toby jugs; Coalport, Crown Staffordshire, Royal Doulton and Royal Worcester "Florals" and "Cottages."
    Crystal, ceramic and silver-plated candlesticks, crystal ashtrays, jelly bean jars, vases, etc., by Reidel, Val St. Lambert, Baccarat, Daum, Royal Worcester, Kosta Boda, Orrefors, Stuart, Atlantis, etc.
    Perfume bottles and other objects for the dressing table by Jenny Blair, Kosta and St. Louis.
    China cache pots, vases, teapots, covered boxes, mugs, coasters, bowls, watering cans, rolling pins, condiment sets, etc., by Villeroy & Boch, Portmeirion, Estensi of Italy, Crown Staffordshire, etc.
    Wicker picnic baskets.

Toiletries: Crabtree & Evelyn, etc.

Books: a wonderful book department with an extremely large collection of children's books.

Clothing: Burberrys rainwear and accessories, cashmere and wool sweaters, kilted skirts, etc.

Toys and dolls: Britains scale models, Nisbet dolls and bears, Paddington bears, etc., "Peter Rabbit" tea sets by Royal Doulton.

Collectibles: see items under china, figurines and gift-ware.

And from the fabulous Harrods food halls: teas, jams, preserves, biscuits, etc.

What can we say about one of the world's most famous department stores? . . . It's more than just a store; it's an institution. When in London, you must visit Buckingham Palace, the British Museum and, of course, Harrods. If you haven't time for the trip you can reap the benefits of the vast array of merchandise by mail. Write and ask for anything you want which is made in the United Kingdom. The store probably carries it. There is an enormous china department. We checked on prices for Wedgwood china and they were among the best we've found. A five-piece place setting of the "Wild Strawberry" pattern was 27.55 pounds ($38.50) before the VAT was deducted and shipping was added. This Wedgwood pattern is $115.00 list price here for one place setting. Need we say more?

Checks, money orders and charge cards are accepted.

Illum
Ostergarde 52
Copenhagen 1001
Denmark
Telephone: (011-45-1) 14 40 02
Telex: 19646

China and ceramic dinnerware: Royal Copenhagen, Bing & Grondahl, Dansk, etc.

Crystal stemware and barware: Holmegaard, Kosta Boda, Orrefors.

Silver and stainless flatware and hollow ware by Georg Jensen and others.

Cookware and kitchenware: Stelton stainless steel and acrylic serving pieces, barware and accessories; Nissen hand-crafted woodenware; Morso cast-iron cookware; Eva Trio aluminum cookware.

Jewelry by Georg Jensen, Flora Danica and others.

Collectibles: annual spoons, forks and knives by Georg Jensen and A. Michelsen; Hans Christian Andersen Christmas wall plates, cups and saucers; Christmas plates by Bing & Grondahl.

Figurines: Bing & Grondahl, Royal Copenhagen and Swarovski crystal.

Clothing: Scandinavian knitwear for men, women and children.

Goose-down comforters.

Toys: Lego, dolls in national folk costumes, wooden soldiers, etc.

Illum is a large department store. Ask for what you want. We asked about Royal Copenhagen dinner services. We received a brochure showing all the patterns, but no price list. The store needs to know a pattern name in order to send you a price. Danish

tax of 18 percent will be deducted. Shipping is approximately $2.50 per kilogram (2.2 pounds).
    Checks and credit cards are accepted.

Lane Crawford, Ltd.
Lane Crawford House
G.P.O. Box 83
Hong Kong
Hong Kong
Telephone: (011-852-5) 266121
Telex: 75486 Lane HX

Oriental objets d'art: floor-standing and wall-hanging silk screens, Coromandel screens, porcelain vases.
    Cloisonné vases, bowls, etc.

Figurines and carvings: porcelain, jade, ivory, soapstone, etc.

Giftware: tea sets, covered teacups, lacquerware, fans, jewelry boxes, evening bags, chess sets, etc.

Furniture: rosewood cabinets, dining room sets, plant stands, small tables, etc.; porcelain lamps.

Jewelry: jade, porcelain, cloisonné, etc.

Lane Crawford is a large department and specialty store with several branches. The main store is filled with Oriental treasures and the fourth floor is divided into small shops each specializing in its own collectibles. The store does not have a general catalog but when we inquired about silk screens we received photographs of what was available. The screens ranged in size from a 3-by-4-foot wall-hanging screen to a 6-by-9-foot floor-standing one. A 3-by-6-foot screen with a floral motif was priced at HK$3,350.00 ($430.00). Prices are determined by both size and design.

Shipping multiple screens dramatically cuts the cost. The cost of shipping one 3-by-6-foot screen is HK$1,500.00, but the cost for shipping two is only HK$1,750.00.

Checks are accepted.

Magasin
Kongens Nytorv 13
Mail-Order Department
1095 Copenhagen K
Denmark
Telephone: (011-45-1) 114 433
Telex: 15975 mdn dk

China and ceramic dinnerware: Royal Copenhagen, Dansk, Bing & Grondahl, Arabia of Finland, etc.

Crystal stemware and barware: Holmegaard, Kosta Boda, Orrefors, iittala, etc.

Silver and stainless flatware and table accessories by Georg Jensen and others.

Giftware: beautifully designed Danish and Scandinavian items for the home in glass, silver, stainless, wood, porcelain and ceramics.

Magasin, also known as Magasin du Nord, is one of the largest department stores in Denmark, with a helpful mail-order department. The store will send brochures in response to your questions. In general you will need a second letter for the price, unless you were specific the first time.

Checks and credit cards are accepted.

OY Stockmann AB
Aleksanterinkatu 52
P.O. Box 220, Export Service
SF00101 Helsinki 10
Finland
Telephone: (011-358-0) 176 181
Telex: 124733

Kitchenware: Fiskars knives and scissors, Arabia of Finland cookware and Opa stainless cookware and serving accessories, Hackman cookware.

China dinnerware and oven-to-table ware: Arabia of Finland.

Crystal stemware and barware: Nuutajarvi of Finland, iittala and Humppila.

Stainless flatware by Hackman, etc.

Giftware: Fiskars hunting knives, some with animal-head handles; Nuutajarvi, Humppila and iittala candleholders, hurricane lamps and candlesticks, Irish coffee sets, salad and fruit bowls, pitchers, decanters, vases in all shapes and sizes, trays, ashtrays, art glass paperweights, etc.; aluminum and brass mobiles by Aarikka Oy; ceramic wall hangings by Kalevala Koru; Humppila glass figurines.

Wood items by Aarikka Oy: wall plaques, bird and animal figures, candelabra and candleholders, picture frames, key rings, pen and pencil holders, bar acces-

sories, children's clothes hangers and animal banks, kitchen accessories and trays, Christmas tree ornaments, Santa and other salt shakers and pepper mills, mobiles, toys and games.

Wood toys and games: crib and playpen learning toys for the infant and toddler, wooden board games and puzzles for the family.

Linen by Finlayson, especially hard-to-find duvet covers.

Jewelry: modern sculptural gold and silver jewelry by Lapponia, jewelry by Sten & Laine.

Specific brochures are available in response to a request, but there is no general catalog. The store is eager to be of service and if there is something made in Finland which is not listed, ask for it.

You can give your home and tree a distinctive look at yuletide with beautiful wooden Christmas bells, hearts, birds, angels, elves and apples by Aarikka. These would also make wonderful gifts.

The Finnish VAT of 16 percent will be deducted from your purchase.

Payment may be made by bank draft or credit card, but you must include a photocopy of each side of your card.

Shannon Mail Order
Shannon Free Airport
Ireland
Telephone: (011-353-61) 62610
Telex: 24049 SMAR EI

Crystal stemware and barware: Galway, Cavan, Edinburgh of Scotland, Tyrone and Waterford.

China and ceramic dinnerware: Belleek, Royal Tara, Adams, Aynsley, Coalport, Mason, Royal Doulton, Royal Worcester, Spode and Wedgwood.

   Children's china: Wedgwood's "Peter Rabbit," Royal Doulton's "Bunnykins," Royal Worcester's "Cabbage Patch" and Coalport's "Paddington Bear."

Giftware: Caithness crystal paperweights, Nobless crystal figurines, Kristal Elegance figurines, Wedgwood Jasperware, china banks, porcelain mug sets, Aynsley gift items, Belleek vases, candy dishes, etc., Limoges gift items; Clarenbridge crystal birthday plates, pewter tankards, trays and punch bowl sets; pewter blazer buttons; chess sets, music boxes, Swiss Army knives, carriage clocks, bone china telephones, decanter sets, perfume bottles, atomizers and vanity sets; blackthorn walking sticks and a take-along seat stick; meerschaum and briar pipes by Peterson.

Figurines: Royal Doulton and Coalport "ladies" and "bunnies," Beatrix Potter and Thelwell series by Beswick, Hummel and Goebel figurines, Border Fine Arts and Anri wood carvings, Nao by Lladro.

Collectibles: Toby jugs; "cottages" and "villages" by Coalport, Lilliput Lane and Wade; Bing & Grondahl collectors' plates; crystal animals and paperweights, Nisbet dolls (also see Figurines above).

Linen: Irish linen handkerchiefs, tablecloths and napkins; Nottingham lace tablecloths.

Blankets: Connemara rugs in tartan plaids; Irish wool blankets.

Clothing: Aran hand-loomed sweaters, Fair Isle sweaters, hand-knit hats and scarves, wool kilted skirts in tartan plaids and tweed pleated skirts, wool jackets and capes, ladies' and men's hats in tweeds, knits and sheepskin, sheepskin slippers.

Christmas and religious: Santa jug by Royal Doulton; Christmas plates by Bing & Grondahl and Wedgwood; Christmas tree ornaments by Spode and Anri; Spode's "Christmas Tree" and Mason's "Christmas Village" dinnerware and giftware; holy water fonts by Belleek, Ford Crafts of County Wicklow and Hummel; rosary beads and Celtic cross jewelry; Goebel and Hummel religious figurines: St. Patrick, Holy Child, angels, etc.; Goebel crèche sets, including figurines; Hummel Christmas spoon and bell.

Food: Irish breakfast gift set containing a Royal Tara teapot, Barry of Cork tea and Lynne's Irish marmalade and preserves; Christmas pudding.

French perfumes, toilet water and toiletries.

Meerschaum and briar pipes by Peterson.

Traditional Irish jewelry.

If your plane has ever stopped at Shannon Airport, you will know this shop. When people think about duty-free shopping, they think "Shannon." The store has been doing a mail-order business for the last thirty-two years through the comprehensive catalogs which arrive in your mailbox several times a year. If you don't see the piece you want in the current catalog, it doesn't hurt to write to ask for the item you are seeking.

Two items that we thought made exceptional gifts were the Irish breakfast set ($28.70) for the tea drinker, and the seat stick ($53.50) for the sports observer or anyone who has to stand and wait outdoors.

Here are some of our price comparisons: The Waterford "Alana" goblet is $30.00 plus $2.55 shipping compared to $45.00 plus tax here. The Waterford celery dish we priced is $64.00 plus $6.95 shipping compared to $101.00 plus tax here. The Royal Doulton "Bunnykins" three-piece set is $18.50 plus $6.25 shipping compared to $36.00 plus tax locally. Prices are in U.S. dollars and mailing charges are clearly stated for each item.

Checks, money orders and credit cards are accepted.

Takashimaya
2-4-1 Nihombashi, Chuo-Ku
Export Department
Tokyo 103
Japan
Telephone: (011-81-3) 211 4111
Telex: J24810 Takstore

China dinnerware, tea services and accessory pieces in both Western and Japanese styles.

Lacquerware: trays, coasters, covered boxes, bowls and bowl sets, plates and plate sets, etc.

Dolls: geisha girls in various poses on lacquered wood bases, some in glass cases. They are approximately 18 inches tall.

Furniture: rosewood and lacquer dining-room sets and occasional pieces.

Giftware: porcelain or lacquer chopstick rests, napkin rings, rectangular and fan-shaped tempura plates and sushi sets; sets of stacked porcelain boxes with a top cover; rice bowl sets in wood storage boxes, Imari ware, obis (kimono sashes); hand-painted, gold- or silver-leaf, silk and lacquer fans.

Takashimaya is a well-known department store. It does not have a general catalog, but will send brochures or pictures of the items you have requested. We have been fascinated by geisha dolls ever since we received one as a gift. An 18-inch-tall doll in full costume is from 6,000 to 12,000 yen ($30.00 to $60.00). Shipping is additional. These dolls are not children's toys; they are collectors' items.

Sending for whole sets of Western-style china is not recommended as we feel you can do better at home. However, the unusual shapes of Japanese-style china and lacquerware are not always easy to find locally. These pieces may be worth your while and would also make wonderful gifts. You can use chopstick rests as knife rests and rectangular tempura plates are wonderful for sandwiches or hors d'oeuvres. By the way, you will notice that Japanese sets always come in service for five as the number four has negative vibes.

Payment is accepted by bank check in yen.

Yue Hwa Chinese Products Emporium
301-309 Nathan Road
Kowloon
Hong Kong
Telephone: (011-852-3) 840 084
Telex: 37195 YHCPE HX

China dinnerware, tea services and serving accessories in both Oriental and Western styles: soup tureens, spoons, rice bowls, etc.

Giftware: porcelain ginger jars, vases, flowerpots; covered mugs; wooden bases and plate stands; cloisonné vases, bowls, display plates, napkin rings, boxes, coasters, etc.
  Red and black carved cinnabar lacquer vases, ashtrays, covered boxes, incense burners, etc.
  Lacquerware vases, coffee sets, wine sets, smoking sets, boxes and napkin rings.
  Jewelry boxes of embroidered silk and also rosewood with brass; framed pictures.
  Stuffed satin embroidered toys, some with loops for hanging.
  Semiprecious-stone floral trees.

Figurines and carvings of ivory, wood, cork, soapstone and jade.
  Shihwan figures and animals (pottery).

Oriental rugs with Chinese designs.

Furniture: rosewood chairs, tables, garden stools, cabinets and breakfronts; Coromandel, inlaid and silk screens and wall hangings.

Linens: tablecloths, placemats, napkins and runners in lace, embroidered linen, cotton and organdy; drawnwork.

Clothing: jackets, blouses and dressing gowns in embroidered silks and satins; petit-point, beaded and embroidered evening bags.

Fabrics: embroidered and printed silks and satins; woolen, cashmere and gabardine suitings.

Jewelry: cloisonné, jade, ivory, turquoise, coral, agate, lapis, cinnabar, enamel and porcelain necklaces, bracelets, rings, pendants, etc.

This is another large department store stocked with merchandise made in China, and the first of the Chinese stores to set up a mail-order department. Once you have specified what items you want from the catalog, the store will send you the specifics of price and shipping. The catalog that was sent for reference had outdated prices and postage charges. Insurance is additional and must be requested if you want it.

One thing we didn't see in the catalog was silk flowers, but we purchased a suitcaseful when we were there in person. They cost a fraction of what you pay here. They are lightweight and crushproof. Football chrysanthemums were a particularly good buy. We bought a dozen.

Bank checks, money orders and credit cards are accepted.

For more department stores, *see*

A. B. Nordiska Kompaniet
The General Trading Co.
Icemart
Switzer & Co.

Fabrics
and Yarns

FOR THE DO-IT-YOURSELFER!
You can knit your own sweaters or sew a closetful of
beautiful clothing with supplies from these sources.

Liberty & Co., Ltd.
Regent Street
London W1R 6AH
England
Telephone: (011-44-1) 734 1234
Telex: 295850

Liberty of London fabric for the do-it-yourselfer.

Fabulous Liberty print fabrics are available by mail
for you or your home. The store will send you sample
swatches if you specify the type of fabric you are
interested in and what you plan to use it for. You
might also indicate your color preferences. VAT will
be deducted from the prices, which run about 30
percent below U.S. prices to begin with.

Postage is additional and payment may be made
by bank draft in pounds sterling or by credit card.

For more fabric and yarn, *see*

Antartex, Ltd.
Brown Thomas & Co.
Casa Quintão
Cash & Co., Ltd.
China Handicraft Co., Ltd.
China Products Co. (H.K.), Ltd.
Chinese Arts & Crafts, Ltd.
Chung Kiu Chinese Prod. Emporium
Cleo, Ltd.
Fallers, Ltd.
Galeries Lafayette
Harrods
Husfliden of Bergen
Icemart
Kevin & Howlin, Ltd.
Kinlock Anderson & Son
Shannon Mail Order
St. Andrews Woolen Mill
Tiroler Heimatwerk
W. Bill, Ltd.
Yue Hwa Chinese Prod. Emporium

Figurines

piece. A small animal starts at about $20.00. A figurine
of two people can be as high as $800.00.

Checks are accepted.

> **Den Kongelige Porcelain Factory**
> **Amagertorv 6**
> **1005 Copenhagen K**
> **Denmark**
> **Telephone: (011-45-1) 13 71 81**

*Underglaze porcelain figurines: people at occupations,
children at play, satyrs, "Little Mermaid," birds, wa-
terfowl, barnyard animals, household pets, forest animals, polar bears, etc.*

Giftware: vases, ashtrays, plaques, boxes and plates.

*Collectibles: yearly plates, picture frames and mugs;
mother and child plates and Hans Christian Andersen
fairy-tale plates.*

China dinnerware and serving pieces.

All items are Royal Copenhagen porcelain. The store
has a catalog and leaflets with prices in Danish kroner.
These charming figures vary greatly in price depending on the size and complexity of the figurine. A
figurine entitled the "Goose Girl" is approximately
$180.00 compared to $385.00 in a popular U.S.
catalog. Likewise, the 7-inch "Polar Bear" is approximately $127.00 if you send for it, compared to
$310.00 here.

Royal Copenhagen is equally well known for its
fine dinnerware, from the charming "Blue Fluted"

WHETHER YOU FANCY FIG-
urines made of porcelain, jade, wood or ivory, you
will certainly like the financial figures from the following shops.

=

Dahl-Jensens Porcelain Works
Frederikssundsvej 288
2700 Copenhagen
Denmark
Telephone: (011-45-1) 280 397

Collectible porcelain figurines: ethnic figures, animals,
birds and children; Hans Christian Andersen fairy-tale
figures.

The catalog shows a large selection of figurines, but
this is only a small part of what is available. This
company has been manufacturing its collectible Danish underglaze porcelain figurines for approximately
sixty years. There is limited production of each
figurine.

Danish export taxes will be deducted from the
prices, which are in Danish kroner. The price range
varies depending on the complexity and size of the

pattern to the elegant and elaborate "Flora Danica" pattern created for Catherine the Great of Russia.

The VAT of 18 percent will be deducted from the listed prices. Postage and insurance are additional.

Checks are accepted.

Kreisler
Serrano, 19
Madrid 1
Spain

Lladro figurines and lamp bases.

This shop has one of the largest selections of Lladro in Madrid. A large brochure and price list are available. You must specify whether you want the shiny or the matte finish. Almost all prices include shipping and insurance via international parcel post. Delivery takes from seven to ten weeks. The shop will send gift items directly to the recipient if you wish.

Checks are accepted.

Roittner KG
Getreidegasse 8
P.O. Box 131
A-5010 Salzburg
Austria
Telephone: (011-43-662) 42566

Figurines by Hummel and crystal animals by Swarovski.

China dinnerware and gifts: Villeroy & Boch, Rosenthal, Gmunder Keramik and Arzberg.

Glassware and barware.

Crystal giftware by Swarovski: candleholders, paper-weights, picture frames, candy and trinket boxes, dinner bells, pendants, whiskey glasses, chess sets, salt and pepper sets and various vases and bowls.

This is another source from J.B.'s last trip. J.B. said the store did not have any brochures but that Roittner's is a three-story store and you can just ask for what you want.

We wrote and asked for what we wanted and received several brochures along with the price quotes we requested. The store deducts the VAT and adds packing, postage and insurance charges to the prices, which are in Austrian schillings. There is a worldwide parcel post and airfreight service for your purchases.

Payment by credit card is preferred.

> **Weiner Porzellanfabrik Augarten**
> **Schloss Augarten**
> **P.O. Box 76**
> **A-1021 Vienna II**
> **Austria**
> **Telephone: (011-43-222) 33 45 81**

Spanish Riding School figurines.

These are the famous white "dancing" horses of Vienna. There is a brochure showing the eight models available in the collection. The "Levade Without Rider" is approximately $370.00, including insurance and airmail postage. If the piece you want is out of stock, delivery may take up to three months.

The prices are in Austrian schillings. Checks (or preferably bank drafts) are accepted.

For more figurines, *see*

A. B. Schou
A. H. Riise Gift Shops
A/S Porsgrunn Porselen
Art et Sélection, s.p.r.l.
Baccarat
Bing & Grondahl
Brown Thomas & Co.
Cash & Co., Ltd.
China Handicraft Co., Ltd.
China Products Co. (H.K.), Ltd.
Chinacraft of London, Ltd.
Chinese Arts & Crafts, Ltd.
Chung Kiu Chinese Prod. Emporium
Cristal Lalique
Csemege-Hungarian Intertourist Shops
Emerald
The English Shop
Fallers, Ltd.
Galeries Lafayette
Harrods
Illum
Lane Crawford, Ltd.
Little Switzerland
Michael Kuchenreuther
Michel Swiss
Nymphenburg Porzellan
OY Stockmann AB
Rasper & Sohne
Reject China Shops

Saxkjaers
Scandinavian Center
Shannon Mail Order
Steigerwald
Tiroler Heimatwerk
Yue Hwa Chinese Prod. Emporium

All Things Floral

SILK FLOWERS, BULBS,
flower-arranging materials: Take your pick!

Franz Roozen
Vogelenzangseweg 49
2114 BB Vogelenzang
Holland
Telephone: (011-31-2) 502 7245

Beautiful bulbs: tulips (all types), hyacinths, daffodils, miniature daffodils, narcissi, anemones, irises, crocuses, muscari, allium gigantheum, etc.
Bulbs for forcing: amaryllis, tulips, narcissi, paper whites and hyacinths.

Walking through the Roozen bulb fields was an unforgettable experience, and thanks to the mailing service we are able to enjoy these beautiful flowers at home every year. In fact, you can't carry the bulbs home with you; they must be sent at the proper time for planting.

The catalog is available in the early summer. You must order before September 15 in the United States and before September 1 in Canada. The bulbs will arrive in October or November. Each variety is packed and labeled separately and planting instructions are included.

Bulbs make wonderful gifts and this company is happy to send gift packages to the lucky people on your list.

There is a minimum order of $14.00. Checks are accepted.

Sogetsu School
2-21 Akasaka 7-chome
Minato-ku
Tokyo 107
Japan
Telephone: (011-81-3) 408 1126

Japanese flower-arranging material, tools and instructions.

Flower containers: porcelain, ceramics, ceramics in bamboo baskets, plastic, glass and lacquer; lacquer boards to place under the various containers.

Needlepoint holders, scissors and Ikebana instruments.

Books: many books on flower arranging.

Ikebana Sogetsu magazine, available by subscription.

Sogetsu is a Japanese school of flower arranging. There is a comprehensive catalog and price list that made us want to drop what we were doing and head for the local flower shop.

Prices are given in yen. Checks are accepted.

For more floral items, *see*

China Products Co. (H.K.), Ltd.
Chinese Arts & Crafts, Ltd.
Chung Kiu Chinese Prod. Emporium
Yue Hwa Chinese Prod. Emporium

Food

SACHER TORTE, AUTHENTIC *baumkuchen*, English tea and biscuits and other goodies can grace your table from the stores listed below.

Alois Dallmayr
Dienerstrasse 14-15
8000 Munich 1
Germany
Telephone: (011-49-89) 22 81 11
Telex: 05-23 615

Food: candy, cookies, cakes, caviar, canned specialties, etc.; teas and coffees; gift assortments of your choice. *Christmas stollen and* **baumkuchen**.

Giftware: chrome and brass bar accessories, tankards, condiment sets, ceramic vases, etc.

Collectibles: art glass paperweights.

Silver hollow ware and gift items: caviar servers, champagne coolers, trays, candlesticks, fruit bowls and candy dishes, salt shakers and pepper mills, etc.

China dinner, tea and coffee services.

We had read about Dallmayr's famous *baumkuchen* (a tree cake) and thought we'd like to try it. . . . So we wrote and asked for two. We received a price list in deutschemarks, and a postal chart. Everything came written in German but we had no trouble choosing what we wanted and figuring out how much the postal charge would be. We sent a check along with our order. Shortly thereafter there arrived two *baumkuchen*, in excellent condition. It was fun serving something unusual to company. The prices with shipping are in line with prices in American fancy-food catalogs.

A general gift catalog is available but if you don't see what you want, ask. The staff is very helpful and the store itself carries a large variety of foodstuffs and other items.

Checks are accepted.

Ceylon Tea Bureau
115 Gunnersbury Lane
Acton
London W3 8HQ
England
Telephone: (011-44-1) 993 2237
Telex: 268141 Metamak G

Ceylon teas, loose and in teabags.

The tea bureau sent us a price list of the teas available and a postage chart. The postage may be more than the cost of the tea, as the teas are very well priced. You and a friend might want to place one order together.

The "Tea Plucker B.O.P." blend is very similar to

an Earl Grey or English Breakfast tea and costs only
1.25 pounds sterling ($1.75) for 8.82 ounces. A 3.30
pound economy-pack blend is 4.99 pounds sterling
($7.00). Postage for 2 kilograms (4.4 pounds) is 5.95
pounds sterling ($8.33).

Checks and postal money orders are accepted.

Konditorei Kreutzkamm
Postfach 50
8000 Munich 1
Germany
Telephone: (011-49-89) 93 11 06

Food: Easter eggs and breads, tortes, marzipan,
baumkuchen, *cookies and candies; also gift assort-*
ments and even an Easter bread for diabetics.

This world-famous bakery, which has been in business
since 1825, has a small catalog with pictures and
prices. Everything is written in German, but the
pictures make it easy to place an order. Gift packages
can be sent for you.

Prices are in deutschemarks and postage is additional.

Checks are accepted.

Fauchon
26, place de la Madeleine
75008 Paris
France
Telephone: (011-33-1) 4742 6011
Telex: 210518

Gourmet food items: caviar, pâté, fish butters, sauces, truffles, flavored mustards, unusual oils and vinegars, herbs and spices, etc.

*Vacuum-packed cheeses. (*NOTE: *Fresh cheese cannot be shipped to the United States because of customs regulations.)*
Cakes and cookies, candies and teas, picnic baskets.

Clothing: scarves, neckties, handbags and totes with the Fauchon logo.

There is a general catalog with price list and shipping charges. Everything is in French.

Browsing through this catalog brought back vivid memories of wonderful lunches. The store has an uncomfortable, stand-up lunch counter at which people fight for a place to eat. The place is always mobbed. The take-out departments are equally busy, but the food is worth the wait. We always buy our picnic lunches here.

They deduct 5½ percent VAT. Shipping charges are additional.

Checks are accepted.

In case you are in the neighborhood, it is located right across from the Madeleine church.

> **Hediard**
> **5-11, rue Jules-Ferry**
> **92400 Courbevoie**
> **France**
> **Telephone: (011-33-1) 4788 6262**
> **Telex: 630 268 F**

Food: candy, candied fruits, fruit jellies, marzipan; foie
gras and caviar; jams, honeys, vinegars and mustards.
  Assorted teas.
  Gift packages.

Hediard has a lovely selection of food and wine, but
remember, you can't send for the wine or liquor, or
even gift packs that contain a bottle of the above.
Items like smoked salmon may only be imported if
they are in sealed (cryovac, or tinned) containers.
   The catalog describes everything in French and the
prices are in French francs. The pictures speak for
themselves, but a knowledge of French would be very
helpful.
   You wouldn't want to stock your shelves here, but
these items would make interesting and unusual food
gifts for the holiday season.
   Checks are accepted.

> **Hotel Sacher Confiserie**
> **Philharmonikerstrasse 4**
> **A 1015 Vienna**
> **Austria**
> **Telephone: (011-43-222) 52 55 75**
> **Telex: 1/12520**

The original and world-famous **Sacher torte.**

This chocolate cake was invented by a young chef in
the service of Prince Metternich. His name was Sacher
and his son is still making this celebrated specialty.
The shop sells from two hundred to four hundred
tortes each day. Many of these are sent to Paris,
London, et cetera, and they can even be sent to you.

Each *torte* is packed in a reusable wooden box and sent to you by air the moment your order arrives. We received our *torte* eleven days after we mailed our order, with a check, to Vienna.

The *Sacher torte* is traditionally served *mit Schlag* (with whipped cream).

The *torte* is available in four sizes and prices are given in U.S. dollars. We ordered the #II which was $29.00, including packing and airmail shipping, and easily served ten. This would make a memorable gift, one which is not seen in every fancy-food catalog you come across.

Checks and money orders are accepted.

For more food, *see*

Cash & Co., Ltd.
Fallers, Ltd.
Harrods
Shannon Mail Order

Furniture

Be it for an apartment or a mansion, look here for that special piece.

A. Gargiulo & Jannuzzi
Piazza Tasso
80067 Sorrento
Italy
Telephone: (011-39-81) 878 1041

Inlaid wood furniture: tables, chairs, chests, desks, game tables and tea carts.

Gift items: inlaid game boards, cigar and card boxes, trays, bookends and wood pictures.

Embroidered linen, lace.

This is the oldest inlaid-wood working factory in Sorrento. Brochures of the beautiful merchandise came with prices that included shipping.

Every item is handmade of rosewood, mahogany, walnut, briar and other fine woods. An inlaid-wood card box to hold two decks of cards would make a fine gift at $20.00.

A set of three nesting tables, with inlaid lids that

lift up for storage, is $390.00, including insurance and shipping.

Personal checks are accepted.

Fundação Ricardo do Espírito Santo Silva
Largo das Portas do Sol 2
Lisbon 2
Portugal
Telephone: (011-351-1) 862 184

Museum-quality furniture and art ornament reproductions.

Portuguese Arraiolos rugs.

Hand-tooled and handmade leather bookbindings.

This is a decorative-arts school and workshop. It is also a museum. The workshop produces copies of famous pieces of furniture using the very same methods and construction techniques employed in making the originals.

Along with a small brochure and price list, we received a list of references that reads like *Who's Who*. As we said before, this is museum-quality furniture for those of you who are looking for something out of the ordinary.

Illums Bolighus
Amagertorv 10
DK 1160 Copenhagen K
Denmark
Telephone: (011-45-1) 14 19 41
Telex: 15879 ilbokh dk

Contemporary Scandinavian furniture.

Down comforters.

China dinnerware and serving accessories: Royal Copenhagen, Dansk, etc.

Crystal: Orrefors, Holmegaard, etc.

Giftware: Dansk brand items, wooden salad bowls, cheese boards, trays, etc.; stainless-steel serving accessories.

Scandinavian cookware.

Rya rugs.

This home-furnishings store is the Center of Modern Design in Copenhagen. There is no general catalog, but the store will respond to your individual inquiry. Prices are given in both Danish kroner and U.S. dollars. VAT will be deducted on anything shipped out of the country. A 46-ounce, 80-by-80-inch goose-down comforter is $198.00 including postage and insurance. This is the most dense comforter we have found, and at a saving of about 33 percent over U.S. prices.

Checks and credit cards are accepted.

J. L. George & Co.
D-9, 2nd floor
Sheraton Hotel
Kowloon
Hong Kong
Telephone: (011-852-3) 690 958

Custom-made teak Coromandel furniture: cabinets, tables, screens, blanket chests, garden stools, plant containers and stands.

J. L. George does not have a catalog, but in response to your specific inquiry, the shop will be happy to send you photographs of what is in stock. If you have a picture of something you like, send it and it can be made up to your specifications.

A 24-by-14-by-36-inch cabinet with a removable shelf was $300.00. A 42-by-36-inch, four-panel Coromandel screen with a gold-leaf background was $150.00. Insurance was an additional $25.00, and shipping to Newark, our nearest port of entry, was $120.00 for both pieces. In our experience, shipping two pieces usually costs the same as shipping just one.

We had a cabinet and a garden stool made up and were very pleased with the results. We were able to choose the color, celadon green, and the Coromandel design we wanted on the garden stool and we were able to have a cabinet made to the exact size needed for a little nook in the entrance hall. We were also able to choose the hardware we wanted. Two of our friends have also had cabinets made up and they were satisfied as well.

Checks or credit cards are accepted.

For more furniture, *see*

China Handicraft Co., Ltd.
China Products Co. (H.K.), Ltd.
Chinese Arts & Crafts, Ltd.
Den Permanente A/S
The General Trading Company
Lane Crawford, Ltd.
Yue Hwa Chinese Prod. Emporium

Gifts

WHAT TO GIVE IS ALWAYS A challenge and often the price tag looms large in the decision. Everything in this book can actually be considered a gift—whenever we saw something of particular interest we tried to mention it in the commentary—but the following may be a perfect collection of ideas for the undecided.

A. H. Riise Gift Shops
37 Main Street
P.O. Box 6280
St. Thomas
U.S. Virgin Islands 00801
Telephone: 1-800-524-2037

Gifts: Bilston & Battersea enamel boxes, Toby jugs, Bossons' heads, Liberty of London accessories, Crabtree & Evelyn toiletries and foods, Wusthof knives, Bing & Grondahl plates, Swatch watches, etc.

Figurines: Bing & Grondahl, Royal Copenhagen, Royal Doulton, Lladro, Baccarat, Daum, Herend, Swarovski, etc.

China: Coalport, Royal Crown Derby, Royal Doulton, Royal Worcester, Christofle, Ginori, Royal Copenhagen, Herend, Wedgwood, etc.

Crystal: Baccarat, Lalique, Orrefors, Swarovski, Daum, Schott-Zweisel, etc.

Jewelry and watches: Patek Philippe, Concord, Ebel, Heuer, Gucci, Seiko, Swatch, Orbit, etc.; Schatz clocks, Ilias LaLaounis gold jewelry, Majorica pearls (those fabulous fakes), Mikimoto pearls (the real thing), Roman coin jewelry.

Clothing: sweaters by Braemar, Barrie, Lyle & Scott, etc.; wool kilts, stoles, etc.

Perfumes and toiletries.

A. H. Riise is really a series of shops within a shop. It is quite convenient to shop here as there is a toll-free number. When we called and asked for what we wanted we were asked to call back in an hour. This allowed time to get all the information for us.

The savings varied from nominal to substantial. We found a large saving on the new Swarovski crystal chess set with mirrored chessboard, available from A. H. Riise for $428.00 plus postage compared to $950.00 plus tax locally. This would make a super gift for the chess player in your life or a great status symbol for your coffee table.

This is also a good place to try if you can't find a source in the country of origin. The Greek goldsmith Ilias LaLaounis will not export individual pieces of his jewelry, but you can buy it here at Greek Gold.

Herend china is another hard-to-find brand. This store carries a selection of soup tureens, gift pieces, figurines, tea services, etc. There were some china services in stock and anything else could be ordered. A five-piece place setting of the "Rothchild Bird" pattern is $145.50 plus shipping compared to $202.00 plus tax on the U.S. mainland. The "Rothchild Bird with Blue Border" is $313.00 compared to $579.00 at home. There is approximately a 20 percent saving on a small Herend animal after you add the $5.00 minimum mailing charge. The percentage saved is greater if several small items are mailed together.

Checks and credit cards are accepted.

Artespaña
Velázquez, 140
Madrid 6
Spain
Telephone: (011-34-1) 411 1362
Telex: 23235 ENAR-E

Gifts: painted and lace fans.
  Brass flowerpots, tea kettles, braziers, tankards, serving spoons, lamps, etc.
  Faience jugs, umbrella stands, candelabra, candleholders, platters, pitchers, ashtrays, etc.
  Wood obelisks, ducks, whales and other ornamental pieces.

Collectibles: ornamental pistols, rifles, etc.

Artespaña deals in Spanish handicrafts. In response to our specific inquiry we received pages from the general export catalog showing a sampling of the merchandise. A second letter is necessary for prices and shipping information.

The General Trading Company, Ltd.
144 Sloane Street
Sloane Square
London SW1X 9BL
England
Telephone: (011-44-1) 730 0411

Giftware: a large selection of gardening supplies; bridge sets, ashtrays, mugs, wine coolers and coasters, hand-woven Durrie cotton rugs, English pewter picture frames, lamps, stationery and desk accessories, Winnie the Pooh children's linens, boot warmers/dryers, wool-fat soap in gift packs, corkscrews, soufflé dishes and ramekins, Limoges ashtrays and accessory pieces, Georgian library steps, crystal vases and paperweights, etc.

China dinnerware: Royal Doulton, Royal Worcester, Spode, Wedgwood, etc.

Collectibles: antique tea caddies and work boxes, antique furniture, Chaucer's "Canterbury Trail" series figurines by Rye Potteries.

Books: children's and gift books, solve-it-yourself mysteries, garden diaries and cookbooks.

Toys: wood puzzles, stuffed animals and dolls, and wood boats for the bathtub sailor.

Christmas items: stockings and tree ornaments.

This is a large specialty store. It does not have a general catalog except at Christmastime when a gift catalog is published. Specific brochures on various brands of china are available. The antiques department is mentioned in the Christmas brochure, so if this is your interest, it would be worth an inquiry.

Gifts can also be mailed directly to the recipient. Payment may be made by check or credit card.

Little Switzerland
P.O. Box 887
St. Thomas
U.S. Virgin Islands 00801
Telephone: 1-800-524-2010

Jewelry: gold jewelry and gold jewelry set with precious and semiprecious stones in all shapes and sizes.

Pearls and pearl jewelry, semiprecious beads.

Watches: Audemars Piguet, Baume & Mercier, Borel, Chopard, Concord, Ebel, Girard-Perregaux, Heuer, Rado, and Vacheron & Constantin.

China dinnerware: Aynsley, Block, Daniel Hechter, Fritz and Floyd, Hutschenreuther, Rosenthal, Royal Doulton, Royal Worcester, Thomas, Villeroy & Boch and Wedgwood.

Children's china by Royal Doulton and Wedgwood.

Crystal stemware and barware: Atlantis, Baccarat, Daniel Hechter, Daum, Hoya, Lalique, Orrefors, Riedel, Rosenthal, Thomas and Waterford.

Figurines: Baccarat, Goebel, Hummel, Lalique, Lladro and Swarovski.

Hollow ware and flatware in silver and stainless: Capricorn, Christofle, Daniel Hechter, Georg Jensen, Rosenthal, Sabattini and Carl Schmidt.

Giftware: china, crystal and silver in brands listed above; bronze paperweights in fruit and animal shapes, desk clocks set in crystal, candlesticks and candleholders, perfume bottles, cruet sets, soufflé and quiche dishes, covered porcelain boxes, tea sets, vases, wine coolers, caviar servers, napkin rings and baby cups; ceramic "paper" bags in brown or white to use as vases, etc.; Wedgwood and Royal Doulton banks, lamps, etc., for children.

Collectibles: Rosenthal plates; figurines as listed above.

This is a must-have catalog that you can get by calling the toll-free number listed above. This number can also be used for more information or to place an order. The catalog shows only a sampling of the enormous selection available. We shopped there in person recently and were able to compare quite a few prices. We bought a three-piece Wedgwood "Peter Rabbit" children's set as a baby gift for only $14.00. It's $36.00 locally. The Swarovski crystal owl which sells for $85.00 at home was $54.00 in the Little Switzerland shop. A Lalique perfume bottle, "Deux Fleurs," was $57.00 compared to $80.00 at home. The Chopard "Happy Diamond" watches were 33 to 50 percent less than at home.

Postage and insurance are additional.

Payment by check, cashier's check, money order or credit card is acceptable. If you use a personal check there will be a delay of six weeks until your check clears.

This catalog wins our "I Don't Believe It; Isn't It Fantastic Award." This is the perfect gift idea for people who love to entertain and are into the gourmet scene.

This award is given for the Rosenthal ceramic grill table, which comes in either a blue-and-white or brown-and-white pattern. It was designed by Bjorn Wiinblad of Denmark and includes a six-segment table top, grill with spit attachment and six each porcelain-handled skewers and grill forks. It also comes with a flat ceramic cover which fits over the grill in the center and completes the tabletop. It's the ultimate grill and serve. We've never seen anything like it! The price: $3,500.00 to the nearest port of entry. Bon appétit!

Saxkjaers
53 Kobmagergade
1150 Copenhagen K
Denmark

Giftware: Bing & Grondahl "Scenes of Denmark" coaster/ wall plaques; Swarovski silver crystal candlesticks and candleholders; porcelain jewelry by Bing & Grondahl; Bing & Grondahl and Royal Copenhagen vases, plates, candy dishes, bowls and ring holders.

Pewter by Selangor: service plates, pitchers, wine jugs, tankards, vases, candlesticks, salt and pepper shakers and pewter stemmed goblets.

Orrefors crystal: perfume bottles, candlesticks, bowls, etc.

Collectibles: Bing & Grondahl annual dolls, bells, thimbles, figurines, Mother's and Children's Day plates, Christmas plates and bells. The new Bing & Grondahl "Gentle Love" series of four plates.

Porsgrunn of Norway Christmas, Father's and Mother's Day plates.

Royal Copenhagen Christmas greeting-card plates, mother and child annual plates, Christmas plates and annual Christmas cups and saucers; annual mugs; limited edition "Little Mermaid" plate.

Swarovski silver crystal animals.

Georg Jensen annuals: forks, spoons and knives in gold-plated sterling silver with enamel.

A. Michelsen Christmas annuals: forks and spoons in gold-plated sterling silver with enamel.

Solid brass plate hooks and bell stands for your collectibles.

Figurines by Bing & Grondahl and Royal Copenhagen: animals, birds, people and fairy-tale characters.

Christmas items: annual tree ornaments in gold-plated brass by Georg Jensen, fabric Christmas elves for the tree, Christmas elves wreaths, chimes and candleholders and mobiles in brass, annual Christmas glasses illustrating Hans Christian Andersen stories, Christmas decanters, Christmas greeting plates by Royal Copenhagen, in self-mailers, Royal Copenhagen "Angel" candlesticks, etc.

China dinnerware by Bing & Grondahl and Royal Copenhagen.

Crystal stemware and giftware by Orrefors.

This store stocks a complete range of Scandinavian glass and porcelain giftware. There is a general gift catalog but you can also write for specific brochures and/or price lists. Prices in the catalog are in U.S.

dollars and include mailing. The price with airmailing is shown in parentheses.

There is a free gift-mailing service available. There is a 10 percent discount on four or more place settings of china dinnerware and a 15 percent discount on Orrefors stemware if you buy at least six of one size in the same pattern.

The current Bing & Grondahl Christmas plate is $35.00 including postage ($38.00 by airmail). It's $54.50, plus tax, if you buy it locally.

Personal checks and credit cards are accepted.

Scandinavian Center
P.O. Box 187
St. Thomas
U.S. Virgin Islands 00801
Telephone: 1-800-524-2063

Crystal: Holmegaard and iittala stemware and bar-ware, platters, vases, bowls, etc.; Hadelands vases, decanters, bowls and figurines.

China: Bing & Grondahl and Royal Copenhagen dinnerware, figurines, Christmas plates, etc.

Stainless steel: Stelton vacuum (thermos) jugs, trays, children's eating sets, fondue sets, pitchers, teapots.

Also Stelton plasticware and Norsk Stalpress stainless flatware.

Wood by Richard Nissen: salad sets, salt and pepper mills and fondue sets.

Sterling-silver flatware by David Anderson and Georg Jensen. Silver, gold and enameled jewelry by David Anderson, Georg Jensen and Flora Danica.

Georg Jensen watches.

Pipes: Dunhill, Ben Wade, James Upshawl, Larsen, Sheriden and Stanwell.

There is a gift catalog with a price list in U.S. dollars and there is a toll-free number to call for placing an order or requesting additional information on any other Scandinavian merchandise. There is also a complete Georg Jensen jewelry and watch catalog available.

The 1985 Bing & Grondahl Christmas plate is $30.50 in this store compared to $54.50 locally. Plates of some other years are available on request. The price for a five-piece place setting of Jensen's "Acorn" pattern sterling flatware is $535.00 compared to $755.00 in the mainland United States.

Checks and credit cards are accepted. (Personal checks take four weeks to clear.)

Airmail delivery is ten to fourteen days. Parcel post takes eight weeks.

Schweizer Heimatwerk
Rudolf Brun Brücke
8023 Zurich
Switzerland
Telephone: (011-41-01) 211 5780

Gifts: Swiss music boxes.
  Dolls in regional dress.
  Lace and embroidery.

This is a center for regional handicrafts. Most of the articles for sale are one-of-a-kind pieces and therefore there is no catalog. The hand-painted music boxes playing Swiss folk tunes range from 40 to 90 Swiss francs. Fine wood music boxes that play classical music range from 250 to 1,200 Swiss francs (approximately $125.00 to $600.00). Dolls are approximately $21.00 each.

Checks are accepted.

Tartan Gift Shop
96A Princes Street
Mail-Order Department
Edinburgh EH2 2EX
Scotland
Telephone: (011-44-31) 225 5551

Gifts: clan crest shields, tartan lap rugs (blankets), Celtic jewelry, etc.

Edinburgh of Scotland crystal stemware and giftware.

Clothing: kilts, sporrans, tweed jackets and Scottish woolens.

A letter will get you information and prices in pounds sterling. A gentleman's Harris tweed jacket is approximately 66 pounds sterling ($92.40), with the VAT deducted and postage and insurance added.

Checks, international money orders and credit cards are accepted.

Wallach
Residenzstrasse 3
8 Munich 2
Germany
Telephone: (011-49-89) 22 08 71

Gifts: beer steins, wood carvings, crafts and folk cos-
tumes.

A catalog is not available, but we received a photograph of a selection of beer steins with prices in
deutschemarks. The steins start at approximately
$18.00. If you have a picture of the kind of stein you
want, send it with your inquiry. Shipping is about
$5.00 for each stein.
    Checks are accepted.

    For more gifts, *see*

        . . . the rest of the book . . .

Jewelry

F<small>ROM A</small> S<small>WATCH TO THE</small> Crown jewels, you can find it here in this treasure chest of listings of watches, enamels, cameos, pearls, filigree, silver and gold.

IMPORTANT NOTICE: Due to import restrictions, Rolex watches may not be imported into the United States through the mail. Customs agents will either destroy the watch or return it to the sender. (You can bring one Rolex watch back with you when returning to the United States.)

A & G Cairncross Ltd., Goldsmiths
18 St. John Street
Perth, PH 1 5 SR
Scotland
Telephone: (011-44-738) 24367

Jewelry: Scottish freshwater-pearl and gold jewelry.
Brooches, earrings, rings, pins, pendants and cuff-links.

The pearls come in shades ranging from whites, creams and grays to silky golds and lilacs. These pearls come from mussels as opposed to oysters, and the settings are of 9-karat gold. Some of the pieces also include semiprecious stones, and a piece can also be designed to your specifications.

A brochure showing a good selection of lovely pieces is available. A price list, in pounds sterling, was included.

Mailing and insurance are 4.00 pounds additional. Checks are accepted.

A. Alioto
Via Ippolito D'Aste 7-5
16121 Genoa
Italy
Telephone: (011-39-10) 562 616

Filigree jewelry in silver, silver and vermeil, vermeil and enamel and 18-karat gold: pins, bracelets, necklaces, rings and earrings.

A folder showing the intricate, step-by-step process is included with the brochure showing a large selection of the pieces available. A price list in lira is included. There are beautiful butterflies, swans, flowers and insects, animals and birds.

The last time one of us was in Italy we had a hard time leaving without at least one of each, as these make such great gifts. Prices start at under $10.00.

Checks are accepted.

A. Michelsen
Bredgade 11
DK 1260 Copenhagen K
Denmark
Telephone: (011-45-1) 14 02 29

Jewelry: silver and enamel on silver.

Collectibles: Christmas spoons and forks in enamel on gilt sterling silver (vermeil).

Danish artists have designed Christmas spoons for this jeweler since 1910. The dies are destroyed after twelve months; however, some spoons made since 1931 can still be supplied. There is no general catalog but brochures are available.

Prices are in Danish kroner and the VAT of 18 percent will be deducted. Insurance and postage are additional.

Checks are accepted.

Bucherer, Ltd.
Schwanenplatz 5
CH 6002 Lucerne
Switzerland
Telephone: (011-41-41) 509 950

Jewelry: 18-karat gold jewelry, some with precious stones. Freshwater pearls, pendants and ring watches. Gold and silver charms.

Watches: Piaget, Baume and Mercier and Bucherer; Swatch.

Gifts: cigarette lighters and pen and pencil sets by Caran d'Ache, Dior, Les Must de Cartier and Dupont.
  Music boxes.
  Beer steins.

Clocks: hand-painted Swiss clocks, brass carriage clocks, travel and alarm clocks and cuckoo clocks.
  Swarovski crystal figurines, candleholders, ashtrays, etc.

This well-known store will happily mail your purchase anywhere in the world. A general catalog, as well as specific watch catalogs (as mentioned above), is available. Prices are in Swiss francs. Mailing and insurance is about $10.00 for one or two watches. They have a worldwide repair service.

On the Piaget watches that we compared there was a saving of approximately 25 percent.

Checks and credit cards are accepted.

Cardow Jewelers
P.O. Box 400
St. Thomas
U.S. Virgin Islands 00801
Telephone: 1-800-524-2046

Gold jewelry: chains and necklaces, bangle bracelets, men's rings, etc.
  Gold jewelry with precious and semiprecious stones: earrings, rings, bracelets, necklaces, etc., in combination with amethysts, aquamarines, blue topazes, diamonds, emeralds, opals, pearls, rubies and sapphires.

This is a tremendous store with a vast collection of jewelry. It offers an extensive selection in the brochure. Diamond karat weights are given in the brochure, but you will have to inquire about the weight of other stones. Notice the toll-free phone number.

The store claims savings amount to 50 percent or more because of worldwide direct buying, high volume, free-port prices and crafting by their own jewelers. Prices are given in U.S. dollars and seemed quite reasonable when we were there. Hard-to-find opal beads, necklaces, pins and pendants were plentiful at Cardow.

Checks and credit cards are accepted. Credit card purchases over $500.00 must be in writing and must include the expiration date of the card.

Colombian Emeralds International
P.O. Box 6075
St. Thomas
U.S. Virgin Islands 00801
Telephone: 1-800-524-2083

Gold jewelry with emeralds and gold with emeralds and diamonds: earrings, rings, bracelets, necklaces and pendants.

A catalog is available with prices in U.S. dollars. Karat weights of stones are given. Notice the toll-free phone number. Wherever practical, jewelry is set with emeralds from Colombia, but sometimes emeralds from other sources are used. All emeralds are hand-cut. Some designs shown are also available with rubies or sapphires. The shop offers an international certified appraisal with each item sold. Prices go from $40.00

to thousands of dollars. For instance, you can get a pair of emerald-cut, 18-karat, emerald stud earrings, totaling .90 karats, for $450.00.

Checks, money orders and credit cards are accepted.

David Anderson
Carl Johansgate 20
Oslo
Norway

Jewelry: sterling silver and gold in modern Scandinavian design.

Sterling-silver vermeil with enamel; necklaces, bracelets, rings, pins, pendants, cufflinks and earrings in snowflake, seashell, butterfly, insect, bird and flower designs.

Sterling-silver flatware.

Giftware: spoons, forks and assorted table accessories made of sterling vermeil with enamel.

A brochure showing some of the beautiful Norwegian enamel jewelry is available. This is the fourth generation carrying on a family tradition begun in 1876.

Prices are in Norwegian kroner and 16.67 percent VAT will be deducted from the price. Postage and insurance are additional. The price of an enameled pansy was about half the price of a similar one we saw in an American mail-order catalog.

Certified checks and international money orders are accepted.

Galerie Bjorn Weckstrom
Unioninkatu 30
00100 Helsinki 10
Finland

Fourteen- and 18-karat gold, silver and platinum jewelry, some set with diamonds or semiprecious stones: pendants, bracelets, earrings, necklaces, brooches, rings, etc.

This striking sculptural jewelry is by one of Scandinavia's leading designers. Some of the pieces remind us of textured gold nuggets. The shop will send pictures, with prices in Finnish marks, of this unusual jewelry. A pair of 14-karat gold stud "Turret" earrings was $160.00. The VAT of 16 percent will be deducted from this price. Mailing and insurance are additional.
Checks are accepted.

Garrard & Co., Ltd.
112 Regent Street
London W1A 2JJ
England
Telephone: (011-44-1) 734 7020
Telex: 8952365 REGENT G.

Jewelry: gold and platinum, most set with precious gems.
Pearls.
Watches and clocks.
Antique jewelry, one-of-a-kind pieces.

Sterling-silver flatware and hollow ware, new and antique: candelabra, tea services, trays, bowls, salt and pepper sets, wine coasters, etc.; Regent plate hollow ware.

Gifts: sterling picture frames and figurines, wood humidors, crystal and porcelain figurines, desk sets and accessories of semiprecious stone, paperweights, antique enameled and jeweled boxes, gold sculpture.

Special commissions: jewelry, trophies, etc.

Garrard was first appointed Crown Jewellers of England in 1843 and it still holds that appointment. The overseas gift catalog shows some of the spectacular jewelry and gift items available. Most of the items are not for the faint of heart, or purse.

Giovanni Apa Co.
P.O. Box 190
80059 Torre del Greco
Italy
Telephone: (011-39-81) 882 6111
Telex: 720220 APA I

Jewelry: cameos unmounted or mounted in sterling silver or 14-karat gold; brooches, bracelets, earrings, tie clasps, cufflinks and rings.

Coral jewelry: beads, rings, pins, earrings, etc.

We dealt with a branch of this firm when we were in Rome and there is a catalog with photographs of the various styles made available by mail. Each cameo is hand-carved and no two are alike. They are carved on four different kinds of shell, each with its own characteristic coloring. They are available in a variety of sizes, noted in centimeters. When you order from this manufacturer you get to choose the design, the color, the size and the mounting.

There are also special masterpiece cameos, which are signed by the artist.

There are cameos with religious motifs, signs of the zodiac, Roman warriors, flowers and scenics as well as a large variety of ladies' portraits.

Due to fluctuations in the price of precious metals, the store will only quote a price after you have made your choice.

Checks are accepted.

**Greek Gold
P.O. Box 6527
St. Thomas
U.S. Virgin Islands 00801
Telephone: 1-809-774-5294**

Gold jewelry by Ilias LaLaounis of Athens.

While we normally suggest you send to the source, Mr. LaLaounis will not export an order of less than $50,000.00. Those of us with more modest budgets, who love this extraordinary 18-karat and 22-karat gold jewelry inspired by Greek, Byzantine and other ancient civilizations, will find a friend in David Blanchard, the owner of Greek Gold. This little shop is located in the A. H. Riise complex in St. Thomas.

Mr. Blanchard makes a trip to Athens each spring to select the pieces for his shop. At that time, if he does not already have the piece you want, he can include it with his order. He will be happy to send Polaroids of the pieces he has in stock if you describe what you want. A style number or picture from a LaLaounis advertisement or catalog would be the most precise identification to send with your inquiry.

When we were in the Virgin Islands we purchased a magnificent pair of earrings at a 21 percent savings over the price in the LaLaounis store in New York. The percent savings varies with the price of the piece. A more expensive piece will yield greater savings. Mailing expenses are included in the price. The duty on gold jewelry is only 7.2 percent.

Checks and credit cards are accepted.

Gubelin
Place du Molard 1
CH 3011 Bern
Switzerland
Telephone: (011-41-31) 22 54 33
Telex: 32 335

Jewelry and watches: Audemars Piguet, Ebel, Omega and Patek Phillippe.

This well-known Swiss jeweler sent us catalogs and brochures, with price lists, for the above brands. An Omega watch we priced was $1,200.00 in the catalog compared to a price of $1,850.00 for the same watch here. Postage and insurance are additional.

Checks are accepted.

Hans Hansens Solv
Amagertorv 16
DK 1160 Copenhagen K
Denmark
Telephone: (011-45-1) 15 60 67

Gold and sterling-silver jewelry in modern Scandinavian designs: rings, pins, pendants, necklaces, bracelets, etc.

Silver flatware and hollow ware.

Brochures with prices quoted in Danish kroner are available. The store will deduct the VAT and add a postage charge. It is hard to compare prices here as prices vary with the designs. A thin silver bangle bracelet starts at about $52.00, less the Danish VAT.

Checks are accepted.

Heyerdahl
Fridthof Nansens Pl. 6
Oslo 1
Norway
Telephone: (011-47-2) 41 59 18

Jewelry: Norwegian enamel on gold-plated sterling silver in pins, earrings, bracelets, pendants, rings, etc.
Enamel jewelry for children.

Giftware: enamel on gold-plated sterling salt and pepper shakers, dessert spoons and forks, etc.

Sterling and silver-plated hollow ware: coffee and tea sets, trays, bowls, candlesticks, etc.

Brochures with prices in Norwegian kroner are available. The enamel work in the shapes of flowers and birds is extremely appealing and the colors are brilliant. A very pretty 2-inch double pansy pin is approximately $50.00.

Checks are accepted.

K. Mikimoto & Co., Ltd.
4-5-5 Ginza
Chuo-ku
Tokyo 104
Japan
Telephone: (011-81-3) 562 3111
(overseas operations)
Telex: J 25918 MIKIMOTO

Pearls and pearl jewelry.

Pearl necklaces must be identified by length of the strand, size (in millimeters) of the pearl, and overall quality. Quality is determined by the luster, shape and smoothness (freedom from imperfections) of the pearl. Pearls come in different colors which tend to go in and out of fashion and this may also affect the price.

Mikimoto lists three qualities: excellent, very good and good.

A 16-inch strand of 6.5–7mm pearls of excellent quality was priced at $2,116.00, compared to a price of $2,900.00 from the New York store for a 16-inch, 7mm strand of their top quality (#5). The store has already deducted the VAT of 13 percent. Insurance and mailing is an additional $38.00 per strand. We also compared a number of pins and earrings in the catalogs and found an average saving of about one third.

Bank checks (preferably in yen) and credit cards are accepted.

Kalevala Koru Oy
Arinatie 4
00370 Helsinki
Finland
Telephone: (011-358-0) 554 556

Bronze, silver and gold jewelry, some set with semipre-cious stones: necklaces, chains, pendants, bracelets, rings, earrings, pins, brooches and cufflinks.

Gifts: letter openers, key rings, etc.

This company re-creates jewelry worn a thousand years ago. Most of the designs are of Finnish origin and the originals are now in museums.

A catalog of this beautiful and unusual jewelry is available. Prices will be given after you make your selection.

Postage is additional.

Checks are accepted.

Perlas Majorica
Avenida Jaime III #11
Palma de Mallorca
Spain
Telephone: (011-34-71) 22 52 68

Jewelry: fabulous imitation pearls.

A catalog is not available. When we wrote to this firm it responded with a postcard with the price and postage charges.

We asked for a 30-inch strand of 8mm pearls. The price was $65.00 plus $5.00 for postage. An ad in a

New York newspaper showed a 36-inch strand of these same pearls in 8mm for $184.00, a 45-inch strand for $217.00 and a 60-inch strand for $261.00. All plus tax, of course.

Checks are accepted.

Piaget
40 Rue du Rhône
Geneva
Switzerland

The complete collection of Piaget watches.

Numerous watch catalogs, with prices in Swiss francs, are available. The styles range from a basic gold watch with a black leather band, at 3,475 Sw.Fr. ($1,700.00) to a diamond- and emerald-encrusted watch with a band of emeralds and diamonds set in gold, at 395,335 Sw.Fr. ($198,000.00). We compared prices on two watches. One was a ladies' gold watch with a leather band. It had a diamond and onyx striped face and a diamond-studded case. The price from Piaget was 8,685.00 Sw.Fr. ($4,340.00); the same watch was advertised in the *New York Times* for $6,790.00. A ladies' polo-style bracelet watch with alternating gold and diamond stripes was 37,405.00 Sw.Fr. ($18,700.00) in Switzerland, compared to $27,000.00 in the U.S. With the money you save, you can easily afford to fly to Switzerland to pick it up in person.

For more jewelry, *see*

A. H. Riise Gift Shops
A/S Porsgrunn Porselen

Ando Cloisonné
Brown Thomas & Co.
China Handicrafts Co., Ltd.
China Products Co. (H.K.), Ltd.
Chinese Arts & Crafts, Ltd.
Chung Kiu Chinese Prod. Emporium
Datesun Opals Manufactory
Den Permanente A/S
Fallers, Ltd.
Hamilton & Inches, Ltd.
Illum
Kinlock Anderson & Son
Lane Crawford, Ltd.
Little Switzerland
Peter Hertz
Reliable Opals (H.K.) Fty.
S. Baltinester
Saxkjaers
Scandinavian Center
Schilz
Shannon Mail Order
Tartan Gift Shop
Tiroler Heimatwerk
Yue Hwa Chinese Prod. Emporium

Leather

THE LUXURY OF FINE
leather goods can be yours for a fraction of the U.S.
price when you shop abroad by mail.

———————————————————————
———————————————————————
———————————————————————

Hermès
24, faubourg Saint-Honoré
75008 Paris
France
Telephone: (011-33-1) 4265 2160
Telex: 280744 HERMES PARIS

Leather goods and accessories: handbags, wallets, belts;
covered books for the purse, pocket and desk; attaché
and briefcases; hand-sewn luggage; saddles.

Umbrellas and silk scarves.

In response to our inquiry about leather handbags,
we received several photographs. The store included
the prices in French francs, deducted the 13 percent
VAT and added shipping and insurance charges.
The Hermès bag we saw in New York was $1,450.00
plus tax. We loved it even more when we could save
$550.00 by ordering it directly from France.

Checks are accepted.

Schilz
30, rue Caumartin
75009 Paris
France
Telephone: (011-33-1) 4266 4648

Leather goods for horse and rider: saddles, crops, bridles and harnesses; riding boots, riding hats and caps.

Handbags, wallets, briefcases, covered notebooks, change purses, gloves and belts.

Gifts: umbrellas, walking sticks, seat sticks, silk scarves and ties; whiskey flacons (hip flasks) covered in pigskin, brass boot jacks, leather golf and polo bags.

Jewelry for the equestrian in sterling silver, vermeil or gold.

This company started out in 1815 as saddle and harness makers. There is an illustrated brochure with descriptions in French and prices in French francs. You will need a second letter for mailing and insurance information once you have made your selection.

The charming gentleman we spoke to in the store spoke fluent English with a British accent, causing our daughters to think of this store as British.

Checks and credit cards are accepted.

Schneider Riding Boot Co., Ltd.
15d Clifford Street, New Bond Street
London W1X 1RF
England
Telephone: (011-44-1) 437 6775

Leather riding boots, ready-made and made to measure.

There are catalogs of Schneider and Cavallo boots available. Schneider boots start at size three or can be made to measure for an additional charge. A detailed measurement chart for measuring each part of the foot and leg up to the knee is included.

Ready-made Cavallo boots starting at size two are available in eleven different shaft sizes with a variable-height inner sole to ensure proper fit. All styles can also be made to measure for an additional charge. A price list in pounds sterling with the VAT deducted is included with the catalogs.

Checks are accepted.

Silvio Luti & Figlio s.n.c.
28-32r Via Parione N.
50123 Florence
Italy
Telephone: (011-39-55) 287 047

Leather goods: briefcases, luggage, handbags, jewelry boxes, wallets, etc.

A catalog is not available. The store will send drawings or pictures of individual items in stock, or you can send a photo or picture of what you would like to have made for you.

A woman's two-compartment top-zippered leather briefcase, 9 by 15¾ inches with outside zippered pocket is about $125.00 plus $18.50 for mailing. A choice of leather colors is available.

Velvet-lined leather jewelry boxes with trays start

at $45.00 for a 7-by-9½-inch box. Shipping for one box is $14.00.

Checks are accepted.

For more leather, *see*

Burberrys

Lighting
Fixtures

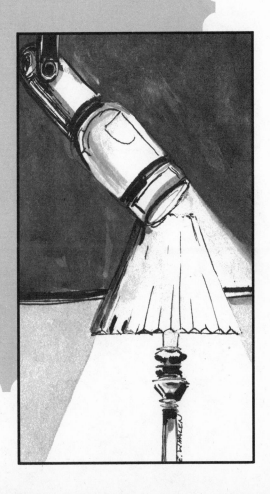

WHETHER IT BE AVANT-garde or traditional, let there be light!

E. Bakalowits Sohne GmbH
P.O. Box 162
A-1171 Vienna
Austria
Telephone: (011-43-222) 52 63 51
Telex: 75806 baka-a

Modern and traditional crystal chandeliers.
Electric candelabra: floor-standing, wall-mounted and for the table.
Table lamps.

Crystal and brass picture frames.

Crystal and glass stemware and giftware.

Herend china.

A catalog showing both traditional and contemporary lighting fixtures is available. Since 1845, Bakalowits Sohne has been providing magnificent lighting for the home or office, the palace or theater, the bank or government building.

Traditional styles have hand-worked iron frames that may be finished in gilt or silver leaf and hung with first quality crystals. Contemporary styles are made of solid brass or high-gloss nickel in a natural brass tone or a true gold-plated finish. The store is willing to make individual designs for special architectural projects.

Deduct 20 percent VAT from prices given in Austrian schillings. Shipping and insurance are additional.

Checks are accepted.

For more lighting, *see*

Brown Thomas & Co.
Cash & Co., Ltd.
Den Permanente A/S
Emerald
Illums Bolighus
Lobmeyr
Shannon Mail Order
Switzer & Co.

Linens
and Lace

ON THE FOLLOWING PAGES you will find shops from which to purchase such items as a monogrammed handkerchief, a lace christening gown, a set of placemats or a 14-foot tablecloth.

Casa Bonet
Puigdorfila 3
Palma de Mallorca
Spain
Telephone: (011-34-71) 22 21 17

Linens: hand-embroidered tablecloths, tea cloths, placemats and napkins.
Men's and ladies' hand-rolled linen handkerchiefs, plain or monogrammed.

The responses and catalogs are mainly in Spanish. The table-linen catalog contains black-and-white drawings of the different patterns available in Mallorcan embroidery. If you know what color embroidery you would like, ask for a sample of the color of the embroidery thread when you write.

Ladies' handkerchiefs start at $1.30 each. There is

a large selection of monogram styles available at an additional charge. After you have made your selection, the store will send prices and shipping information.

Checks are accepted.

D. Porthault S.A.
18, avenue Montaigne
75008 Paris
France
Telephone: (011-33-1) 4720 7525

Linens for bed, bath and table: sheets, pillowcases, pillow shams, bedspreads, towels, terry robes and bathroom accessories, beach towels, tablecloths, napkins and placemats.

Gift items: Limoges tea sets and breakfast sets in patterns to match their linens; plastic trays in coordinating patterns; boudoir pillows, terry turbans, pot holders, aprons, handkerchiefs, bread-basket liners, tea and egg cosies.

Clothing: christening dresses and baby and children's clothes; gown and peignoir sets and men's undershorts.

This world-famous company suggests that you start by sending to its New York store (57 E. 57th Street, New York, N.Y. 10022) for the latest catalog. There is a $2.50 charge for the catalog.

Once you know exactly what you want, the French store will be happy to give you all the necessary information for ordering.

Checks are accepted.

F. Rubbrect
Grand'Place 23
B-1000 Brussels
Belgium

Linen and lace: placemats, tablecloths, napkins, table centers, bridge tablecloths, bread-basket liners, coasters, guest towels, tray cloths and handkerchiefs.

Lace clothing: aprons, wedding mantillas, christening gowns, baby caps, bibs and booties.

A catalog with photographs showing the styles is available. Tablecloths are available up to 170 inches in length. The shop uses only the best-quality Belgian linen, which is available in a variety of colors. It specializes in Brussels lace, called "Luxeuil," and in "Princess Lace," which is lace appliquéd on tulle.

A Brussels lace biscuit and roll cover was $11.00 compared to a similar one we saw for $25.00 in a New York department store.

Placemats range from $6.00 to $37.00 each. A 72-by-108-inch tablecloth with twelve napkins starts at $390.00.

Prices are quoted in Belgian francs and are determined by the amount of lace and the intricacy of the design. Postage and insurance are additional.

Payment is accepted by travelers' check and direct bank transfer. Personal checks are accepted with an $8.00 surcharge for collection.

Madeira House
Rua Augusta 131-135
1100 Lisbon 2
Portugal
Telephone: (011-351-1) 32 05 57

Linens: Madeira embroidered tablecloths, table runners, placemats, napkins, handkerchiefs, etc.

A catalog is not available. Tablecloths are hand-embroidered on linen or organdy. A 70-by-108-inch cloth can cost from $287.00 up to $3,000.00. If you specify the size you need, the fabric you want and the approximate amount you want to spend, you can get pictures of the patterns available.

Shipping is approximately $30.00 per tablecloth. Checks are accepted.

For more linens, *see*

A. Gargiulo & Jannuzzi
Brown Thomas & Co.
Cash & Co., Ltd.
Chinese Arts & Crafts, Ltd.
E. Braun & Co.
Emerald
OY Stockmann AB
St. Patrick's Down
Yue Hwa Chinese Prod. Emporium

Objets
d'art

THIS TERM MEANS DIFFERENT things to different people. Here we have elegant cloisonné, antiques, jeweled treasures and other objects to tickle your fancy. You may also want to look under Figurines, China and Crystal.

Charles & Philippe Boucaud
25, rue du Bac
75007 Paris
France
Telephone: (011-33-1) 4261 2407

Antique pewter: one-of-a-kind pieces for the serious collector; tankards, covered saltcellars, bowls, platters, covered servers, candlesticks, porringers and pitchers.

This firm is one of the foremost specialists in the field of antique pewter. There is a catalog with photos of most of the pieces and any relevant hallmarks. The accompanying text is in French and the prices are in French francs. The store will guarantee, in writing, the authenticity of the objects described in the catalog. At your request you can get a written appraisal for insurance purposes.

Ando Cloisonné Co., Ltd.
6-2, 5 Chome, Ginza
Chuo-Ku, Tokyo
Japan
Telephone: (011-81-3) 572 2261

Japanese cloisonné objets d'art: vases, covered boxes and containers, wall plaques, etc.

Cloisonné jewelry: pendants, necklaces, pins, cufflinks, tie clips and tie pins.

Cloisonné giftware: compacts, cigarette sets, ashtrays, hors d'oeuvre forks and demitasse spoons.
   Trophies and insignia pins.

There is a catalog with photographs of the beautiful Japanese cloisonné pieces. The price list is in U.S. dollars and also indicates the size of each piece as well as the number of pieces of each design that are produced each month.

Japanese cloisonné is very different from Chinese cloisonné in appearance. There is no uniform background of small cells as in the Chinese style. The catalog has a pictorial essay on the manufacture of this artwork. The vases are spectacular and the prices are commensurate with the design quality.

Checks are accepted.

For more objets d'art, *see*

   Alois Dallmayr
   China Handicraft Co., Ltd.
   China Products Co. (H.K.), Ltd.

Chinese Arts & Crafts, Ltd.
Fundação Ricardo do Espírito Santo Silva
Garrard & Co., Ltd.
The General Trading Co.
Lane Crawford, Ltd.

Perfumes and
Toiletries

E. WHALEN

IF YOU LIKE FINE PERFUMES,
you'll save more than cents on these scents.

———————————————————————
———————————————————————
———————————————————————

Manufacturers of perfume are converting to milliliters from grams in countries that use the metric
system. Here is an approximate size guide which you
may find handy for perfumes, toilet water, soaps, etc.

7–7.5 ml. = approx.	¼ oz.
15 ml.	"	½ oz.
28–30 ml.	"	1 oz.
60 ml.	"	2 oz.
100 ml.	"	3⅓ oz.
120 ml.	"	4 oz.
125 ml.	"	4¼ oz.
150 ml.	"	5 oz.
200 ml.	"	6¾ oz.
240 ml.	"	8 oz.

7 grams	=	¼ oz.
14 grams	=	½ oz.
28 grams	=	1 oz.

Michel Swiss
16, rue de la Paix
75002 Paris
France
Telephone: (011-33-1) 4261 6111

Perfume: perfume, toilet water, cologne, soap, bath oil, body lotion, talcum powder, toiletries, etc.

Brands available: Loris Azzaro, Balenciaga, Balmain, Jean Charles Brosseau, Cacharel, Pierre Cardin, Caron, Cartier, Carven, Chen Yu, Courrèges, Jean Couturier, Jean D'Albret, Dana, Alain Delon, Madeleine de Rauch, Jean Desprez, Christian Dior, Fabergé, Roger & Gallet, Givenchy, Grès, Gucci, Halston, Hermès, Jacomo, Charles Jourdan, Karl Lagerfeld, Lancôme, Lanvin, Guy Laroche, Le Galion, Leonard, Molinard, Molyneux, Germaine Monteil, Pascal Morabito, Patou, Robert Piguet, Paco Rabanne, Révillon, Nina Ricci, Rochas, Sonia Rykiel, Jean-Louis Scherrer, Sisley, Torrente, Valentino, Van Cleef & Arpels, Gianni Versace, Weil, Worth and Yves St. Laurent.

Beauty products by Lancaster, Lancôme and Orlane.

Giftware: Marcel Franck atomizers for purse or dressing table, Limoges powder compacts and hand mirrors, designer silk scarves, Sèvres crystal miniatures.

No trip to Paris is complete without a stop to buy perfume, and this is one of our favorite stops. This shop has a twenty-four-page export catalog that is just a sample of what is available and the prices are in U.S. dollars. There is a gift wrap/card service at no extra charge.

Mailing is additional and no more than three 1-ounce bottles of perfume, or one 8-ounce bottle of toilet water or cologne, can be shipped in a single package. This is due to customs and safety regulations. Because of the U.S. trademark regulations, certain brand names may be blacked out by the U.S. Customs Service. This is no way affects the contents.

"Opium" by Yves St. Laurent is $70.30 an ounce at Michel Swiss, compared to $170.00 an ounce at home. One-half ounce of Balmain's "Ivoire" perfume is $48.05, compared to $95.00 at home and you can have both of these perfumes sent home for only $4.00 additional. A 1-ounce spray of Carven's "Ma Griffe" toilet water is $16.00, plus tax, at home; you can get a 4-ounce spray for $20.60 plus $5.00 postage from Michel Swiss.

Personal checks or money orders are accepted.

J. Floris, Ltd.
89 Jermyn Street
London SW1Y 6JH
England
Telephone: (011-44-1) 930 4136

Fragrances for him and her: perfume, toilet water, cologne, bath oils, bath powders, soaps, aftershave lotion and balm, hair oil, shaving soaps and creams, deodorant, brushes, etc.

Fragrances for the home: potpourri, pomanders, scented drawer liners, sachet, room perfume sprays, perfumed candles and vaporizers.

J. Floris has specialized in the finest English flower perfumes since 1730. There is a brochure with prices given in pounds sterling.

We compared prices in the brochure with prices we found locally. A 3½-ounce (100 ml) bottle of toilet water is $22.50 here and $13.65 (9.75 pounds sterling) in the brochure. A 1¾-ounce bottle of toilet water is $19.50 locally compared to $8.35 (5.95 pounds sterling). Soap is another good buy at 3.75 pounds sterling ($5.15) for three bars compared to $11.50 for three bars at home. They deduct an additional 10 percent from these prices on merchandise leaving the British Isles. Postage, packing and insurance charges are additional and depend on the value of your order.

The items for the home would make wonderful house gifts or Christmas presents.

Checks, money orders and credit cards are accepted.

For more perfume, *see*

> Burberrys
> Galeries Lafayette
> Harrods
> Hermès
> Shannon Mail Order

Pipes
and Smoking
Accessories

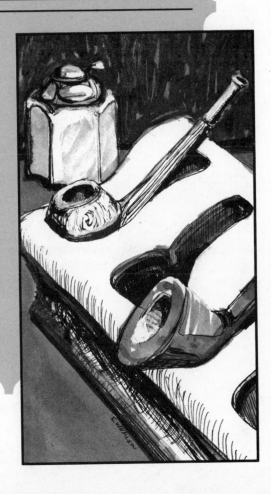

Lɪɢʜᴛ ᴜᴘ ɪɴ sᴛʏʟᴇ ᴡɪᴛʜ ᴀ hand-carved pipe.

Anne Julie's Pibemagerier
Vester Voldgade 8
1552 Copenhagen
Denmark
Telephone: (011-45-1) 129 657

Hand-carved pipes.

There is no catalog but Anne Julie will make any pipe to order if you send a picture of it. She can also send you a few photographs of what she has available if you give her some idea of what you want.

Prices start at 600 Danish kroner (approximately $65.00). Pipes with sterling silver start at 3,000 kroner. These beautiful pipes will be treasured by the recipient.

Checks are accepted.

Hayim Pinhas
P.O. Box 500
Istanbul
Turkey
Telephone: (011-90-1) 522 93 02
Telex: 23 605 Dan Tr.

Hand-carved meerschaum pipes.
Hand-carved meerschaum cigar and cigarette holders.

Hayim Pinhas has been in the pipe business, in Istanbul, since 1938. He offers a fully illustrated catalog of both classic and unusual pipe designs. The origin and care of meerschaum pipes are clearly explained in the catalog.

Prices are given in U.S. dollars and prices for pipes start as low as $10.00. Fitted cases are available for an additional $3.50. There are also gift-boxed sets of two or three pipes.

We particularly liked the interesting "Socrates" portrait pipe which is only $16.00. We ordered this one and another with simpler carving which was only $10.00. They came in five weeks and we think that they compared favorably with pipes we have seen that cost four times as much.

There is a minimum order of two pipes. Airmail is $2.50 per pipe. Checks are accepted in U.S. dollars only!

Mr. Pinhas asks that you type your name and address, or print it clearly in capital letters.

Sommer
11-13-15, passage des Princes
75002 Paris
France
Telephone: (011-33-1) 4296 9910

Handmade, signed, numbered and stamped meer-
schaum (Ecume de Mer) and briar pipes.

Giftware: accessories and leather goods for the smoker.

A brochure is available with a sampling of prices.
Descriptions of the pipes are given in French. Sculp-
tured pipes and special creations are also available.
   Prices start at approximately $65.00. Shipping costs
are additional.
   Checks are accepted.

   For more pipes, *see*

   Cash & Company, Ltd.
   Fallers, Ltd.
   Scandinavian Center
   Shannon Mail Order

Rugs

A LETTER IS YOUR MAGIC carpet to a world of rugs. With a letter and a little bit of patience you can have great savings on a ready-made or made-to-order rug.

Casa Quintão
Rua Ivens 30
1200 Lisbon
Portugal
Telephone: (011-351-1) 36 58 37
Telex: 15494 Seriex P Att Quintao

Handmade wool Arraiolos needlepoint rugs in either coarse or fine weaves.

Rug and pillow kits.

These rugs have been made in homes or convents in or around the town of Arraiolos since the end of the sixteenth century. The original patterns showed a Persian influence; however, today you or your decorator can have any design, color or shape that you wish. If you would like to try your hand at making one of your own, the store sells a rug kit.

There is a catalog showing some of the selection of designs available from this firm, which has been in business since 1880.

These rugs start at approximately $75.00 a square meter for the coarse weave in a stock design. The finer stitch is about 50 percent more.

Shipping is about 15 percent additional and Casa Quintão routinely ships carpets to all parts of the globe.

A deposit of 50 percent is required when the order is placed.

Checks are accepted.

Husfliden of Bergen
3 Vagsalmenning—P.O. Box 416
5001 Bergen
Norway
Telephone: (011-47-5) 21 40 35

Rauma ryer (rya) rugs of 100 percent Norwegian wool. Ryer rug kits.

Hand-knit sweaters, socks, caps, gloves and mittens. Knitting yarns, kits and supplies.

Spinning wheels and folkcrafts.

Brochures showing some of the fabulous designs and colors which can be found in Rauma ryer rugs and rug kits are available.

The sweater brochure shows the many patterns that can be had and the range of yarn colors available. The sweater measurement chart, sent with the catalog, ensures a correct fit.

Prices are given in Norwegian kroner and the shop

will deduct the VAT. Sweater prices range from a child's hand-knit pullover at 190 Nkr. ($25.00) to a man's hand-knit cardigan at 755 Nkr. ($100.00). Postage or freight is additional.

Checks and credit cards are accepted.

Karamichos Mazarakis Flokati
31-33 Voulis Street
Athens 10557
Greece
Telephone: (011-30-1) 322 4932

Handwoven Flokati wool rugs.
  Reversible Kilim wool rugs.
  Berber wool rugs.

A brochure with photos of the various patterns and price list is available, with prices in U.S. dollars. Shipping and mailing charges are also indicated. These rugs are available in a variety of sizes and weights. Extra-thick Flokati rugs, grades 8A and 9A, are available on a special-order basis. All Flokati and Berber rugs are made of long-fiber, New Zealand Drysdale wool.

For the holiday season we received an additional brochure with a special offer in which the prices included airfreight from Athens to New York, duty, and UPS charges for delivery anywhere in the United States. A super bargain! A 5-by-7-foot 4A heavyweight Flokati was $270.00 complete, saving approximately $100.00 in mailing charges and duty.

Checks, money orders and credit cards are accepted.

For more rugs, *see*

Antartex, Ltd.
China Products Co. (H.K.), Ltd.
Chinese Arts & Crafts, Ltd.
Chung Kiu Chinese Prod. Emporium
Illums Bolighus
Tiroler Heimatwerk
Yue Hwa Chinese Prod. Emporium

Silver

Sᴛᴀɪɴʟᴇꜱꜱ, ꜱᴛᴇʀʟɪɴɢ, ꜱɪʟᴠᴇʀ plate and pewter, it's all "silverware" to us. However you choose to set your table, you can expand your options and choose from a wider range of patterns and pieces when you shop by mail.

Christofle
12, rue Royale
75008 Paris
France
Telephone: (011-33-1) 4260 3407
Telex: PAVCHRI 214485

Flatware and hollow ware: silver plate, sterling and stainless.

China dinnerware: Ceralene and Raynaud.

Crystal stemware and barware: Baccarat, St. Louis, etc.

Giftware and accessories: candlesticks and candelabra, salt and pepper shakers and mills, hors d'oeuvres picks, salad servers, dessert sets, fruit bowls, liquor decanter sets, enamel- and brass-handled bar tools, brass wine racks and bottle holders, ice buckets and wine coolers, wine-bottle coasters, tea and coffee services, pitchers, vases, etc.

A brochure with prices given in French francs is available. The store will deduct 15.68 percent VAT on china, crystal and silver plate; 25 percent VAT on sterling silver. Shipping depends on weight and value.

Christofle is famous for quality silver plate, so we compared prices on two patterns. A five-piece place setting of the "Cluny" pattern is $110.00 in the United States and $69.00 by mail. The "Marly" pattern is $125.00 locally, and $78.00 by mail. A silver-plated bar knife we priced from Christofle was $31.00, compared to $55.00 here. A silver-and-wood knife holder for the buffet table was seen for $500.00 in New York, but you can send to Paris and save over 40 percent.

Checks and credit cards are accepted.

Georg Jensen Silver
Ostergade 40
DK 1100 Copenhagen
Denmark
Telephone: (011-45-1) 11 40 80

Sterling-silver jewelry: neck rings and necklaces, pendants, bangle and link bracelets, leather and sterling bracelets, rings with and without semiprecious stones, cufflinks and shirt studs, tie bars and tacks.

Sterling-silver, silver-plate and stainless-steel flatware and hollow ware.

Gifts: key chains and key rings, bookmarks.

Collectibles: annual Christmas tree decorations in brass; gold-plated sterling silver with enamel annual spoons, forks and knives.

This is a quality name which speaks for itself. You may want to visit a store that carries his work before you write, as the store will only send the few pages from the catalog that pertain to your request. Our price comparisons on several bracelets showed a savings of more than 33 percent.

Prices are in Danish kroner and include the 18 percent VAT which will be deducted. Mailing and insurance are additional.

Checks are accepted.

Peter
191, faubourg Saint-Honoré
75008 Paris
France
Telephone: (011-33-1) 4563 8800

Handmade sterling-silver hollow ware: tea and coffee services, trays, bowls, etc.

Cutlery: beautifully made kitchen and professional knives, hunting knives, carving sets, etc.

Monsieur Claude Peter is a master craftsman dealing in the very finest silver. He does not have a catalog but will send you large-size sketches (renderings) of the items you require.

Price lists are in French francs. Shipping and insurance are additional and amount to about $300.00

on a coffee and tea service which sells for about
$4,700.00.

Peter Hertz
Kobmagergade 34
Copenhagen 1150
Denmark
Telephone: (011-45-1) 12 22 16

Handmade sterling-silver flatware.

Sterling and gold jewelry.

This firm has been producing quality Danish tableware and jewelry since 1834. A catalog is available
and the prices, which are in Danish kroner, include
shipping and insurance. A typical five-piece place
setting is priced at approximately $330.00.
Checks are accepted.

Pewter Centre
Ny Ostergade 2
1101 Copenhagen K
Denmark
Telephone: (011-45-1) 14 82 00

Pewter giftware: mugs, candlesticks, candelabra, candle
snuffers, coffee and tea services, candy dishes, bowls,
salt and pepper sets, coasters, etc.

There is no catalog because of the large variety of
merchandise from many different vendors. The shop
carries pewter from the Scandinavian countries and
from Western Europe. The helpful people at the

Pewter Centre will be glad to send you some pictures; but since there are over one hundred different candlesticks for example, we think it would be better if you could send a picture or sketch of what you want.

The shop will deduct the VAT. Shipping and insurance are additional.

Checks, money orders and credit cards are accepted.

Puiforcat
131, boulevard Haussmann
75008 Paris
France
Telephone: (011-33-1) 4563 1010
Telex: Puiforc 640444F

Handwrought sterling-silver flatware and hollow ware: flatware dinner services, candlesticks and candelabra, gravy boats, pitchers, salt and peppers, sugar casters, serving bowls and platters, trays, soup tureens, wine coolers, coffee and tea services, antique reproductions, etc.

This company is continuing a tradition begun in 1820. At the turn of the century the company was collecting the best examples of artistry in silver, most of which can now be seen in the Louvre. Puiforcat has exclusive rights to reproduce this collection, some of which is shown in its catalog. It owns about 180 flatware patterns and 10,000 hollow ware models.

A five-piece place setting of their art deco pattern "Cannes" lists for $930.00 plus tax in New York and can be had, by mail, for $585.00 plus shipping. (The shipping charge for eight place settings is about $80.00).

Payment can be made by check or credit card.

For more silver, *see*

Alois Dallmayr
Art et Sélection, s.p.r.l.
David Anderson
Editions Paradis
Fallers, Ltd.
Garrard & Co., Ltd.
Hans Hansen Solv
Harrods
Heyerdahl
Illum
Magasin
OY Stockmann AB
Rosenthal Studio-Haus
Saxkjaers
Scandinavian Center
Zoellner-Rosenthal Porzellanhaus

Specialties

Hobbyists, do-it-your-selfers, left-handers, musicians and sportsmen, look here first.

Alresford Flyfishers
3 Bakehouse Yard
52B West Street
Alresford
Hampshire S024 9AU
England
Telephone: (011-44-96273) 4864

Flyfishing equipment.
  Shooting accessories.
  Country clothes.

Hampshire is the mecca of flyfishing the world over, and a business associate in Alresford raves about Jack Sheppard and his "Chalk-Stream School of Flyfishing." Jack is a teacher as well as a shopkeeper, and he will be glad to supply your flyfishing needs. He does not have a catalog, but he will be happy to answer your inquiries.

Anything Left Handed, Ltd.
65 Beak Street
London W1R 3LF
England
Telephone: (011-44-1) 437 3910

Articles for the left-handed.

Kitchen and tableware: can openers, vegetable peelers, assorted knives, corkscrews, ladles, pastry servers, Mouli graters, etc.

Scissors: children's safety, paper and teaching scissors; Fiskars kitchen scissors, Wiss dressmaker scissors; all-purpose, embroidery, manicuring and kitchen scissors; tailors' and pinking shears, scissors for hairdressers and nurses.

Stationery items: Osmiroid nibs and pens, Platignum pens, Pelikano pens, Mitchell pen sets, index and address books, greeting cards, playing cards, rulers and T-squares.

Books: **Left-Handed Calligraphy, Left Hand Guitar Book, Teaching Left-Handed Children, Left-Handed Knitting, Left-Handed Needlepoint, Left-Handed Crochet** *and "Helping Your Left-Handed Child to Write" (magazine article).*

Miscellaneous tools: pruning shears, farriers' knives and sailmakers' palms.

A brochure listing the various items is available. All prices are quoted in pounds sterling and include the VAT. Postage and insurance are additional. If your order totals more than 100 pounds sterling, they will give you a 30 percent discount. So, if you have any left-handed friends, you can save by ordering together.

They request two international postage coupons (available at your post office) for their catalog.

Checks are accepted, but international money orders are preferred.

Datesun Opals Manufactory
G.P.O. Box 7201 Central Hong Kong
36-44 Nathan Road
Kowloon
Hong Kong
Telephone: (011-852-3) 722 6789
Telex: 52084 DATOP HX

Australian opals ready for setting, opal beads, carved opal.

This company takes opal from its mine in Australia and transforms it into pieces ready to be set in jewelry, or beads ready for restringing. It also does carvings in opal. A list with prices in U.S. dollars is available. Prices are by karat weight and range from as low as $.30 to as high as $40.00 per karat weight for oval, pear, marquise and round shapes, as well as opal beads.

A follow-up letter may be needed to pinpoint the specifics after you receive the list.

Checks, bank drafts and money orders are accepted.

Mullins of Dublin, Ltd.
36 Upper O'Connell Street
Dublin 1
Ireland
Telephone: (011-353-1) 741 133

Coats of arms plaques, door knockers, insignias, car and blazer badges, heraldic scrolls and Scottish tartan plaques. Heraldic stained glass.

Full-size suits of armor, swords, halbards, medieval weapons and sword trophies.
"Knight" paperweights and letter openers.

No castle is complete without a knight in shining armor and if your "castle" needs a finishing touch for the entry hall or library, how about a 76-inch-tall suit of armor! If something smaller is desired, perhaps a stained-glass window with the family crest would be appropriate.

There is a brochure showing some of the items available. In addition, if you have your own coat of arms, the store will reproduce it on the items produced. You should state the country of origin and alternative spellings of any name required. If there is already a coat of arms in the family, send a sketch or photograph, including colors, as more than one coat of arms may be recorded for some families.

Personal checks and international money orders are accepted.

Musique et Art, S.A.R.L.
141, faubourg Saint-Denis
75010 Paris
France
Telephone: (011-33-1) 4607 0224

Musical instruments: brass and woodwind; French brands such as Selmer, Buffet, Bach, etc.

Last spring when the musical husband was in Paris he bought three Selmer saxophones for about 40 percent of what he would have paid in the music district of Manhattan. So naturally we wrote to the shop. Unfortunately, there was no response to our inquiry, which was in English. If you can write French and are musically inclined, this place is worth a letter. Of course, if you're in town, it's definitely worth a stop.

Reliable Opals (H.K.) Fty.
P.O. Box 90144 T.S.T. Post Office
44A Hankow Road
Kowloon
Hong Kong
Telephone: (011-852-3) 721 8371
Telex: CWDLY 66366 -C/O CHAN 3-721-8371

Australian opals ready for setting, carved opals, opal beads.

A descriptive list is available from this firm which has its own Australian opal mine. Opals of all sizes and shapes are available. Carved opals are a specialty and we received a photograph of what was available.

Except for strands of commercial-grade beads, which are priced by the 16-inch strand, all opals are priced by the karat and the price includes insured air parcel post. As opals have many levels of color and "fire," this company offers an unconditional guarantee of refund or exchange if you are not satisfied with what is sent.

If you are interested in something special, the company will be glad to satisfy your needs. When we inquired about opal beads, we found that those on the list were not what we had in mind. A strand of 7½mm, 20 inches long (estimated at about 105 karats) of high-quality beads is priced at $1,000.00. The same length strand of 4mm blue/green beads, with "lots of fire," is priced at $200.00. These prices seem excellent to us compared to prices of the few available strands we have seen in New York. We decided to order a 16-inch strand of the 4mm beads at $160.00.

The strand of beads arrived within three weeks, duty free, and they compared favorably to any we had seen at more than two to three times the price in the city. Good as they were, we wanted even better and so we returned them by insured airmail and received a lovely letter and a refund check, minus $5.00 for their original postage and insurance, in four weeks. Note that these strands were on strings without clasps and would have had to be restrung before they could be worn.

Payment may be made by bank check or money order.

Schauer & Co.
P.O. Box 13
A-1231 Vienna
Austria
Telephone: (011-43-222) 84 15 43
Telex: 131194

Enamels for the hobbyist: transparent and opaque enamels; ball, thread, mosaic and glitter enamels; special-order enamels.

For those of you who make enamel jewelry or do enamel artwork, Schauer offers 192 colors of enamel including flux, opals, transparents and opaques. This brand of enamel, which is known for its clarity of color, is hard to find in the United States and so we wrote to the source.

There is a brochure showing the complete color palette, and technical information for use of the enamels is given in chart form on the reverse side. A price list in Austrian schillings is included.

Enamels are available in lump or powdered form in 250 gram (.5 lb), 1 kilogram (2.2 lb), 5 kg (11 lb), and 10 kg (22 lb) packages. Threads, balls, mosaics and glitter are available in small quantities.

Special grindings and special colors can also be had from this company.

Packing, shipping and insurance are additional.

Checks are accepted.

Walton's
2-5 North Frederick Street
Dublin 1
Ireland
Telephone: (011-353-1) 47 80 5
Telex: 32932

Musical instruments: Irish harps, flutes, bodhrans, marching drums, bagpipes and accessories; Selmer woodwind instruments.
   Irish sheet music, records and cassettes in both English and Gaelic.
   Irish music and songbooks.

Brochures and catalogs are available. Harp prices are given in U.S. dollars and include packing, insurance and airfreight to the nearest principal airport. Prices for records and books are given in Irish pounds with an additional charge for postage, packing and insurance.
   The records, tapes or music books would make great gifts and you won't find this selection in your local record shop.
   Checks are accepted.

   For more specialties, *see*

   Force 4, Chandlery
   J. A. Henckels Zwillingswerk AG
   Schweizer Heimatwerk

Toys

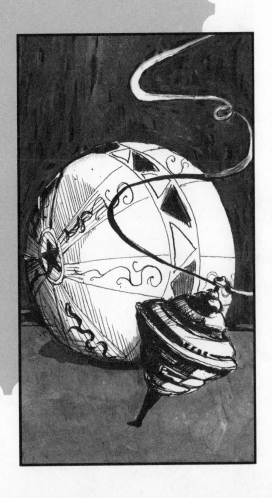

Make someone happy, the young or the young at heart!

Hamleys of Regent Street, Ltd.
188-196 Regent Street
London W1R 5DF
England
Telephone: (011-44-1) 734 3161

Toys: Britains' toy soldiers, knights, Turks, Civil War soldiers, cowboys and Indians, soldiers and military, spacemen and aliens; barnyard and zoo animals; trucks, farm equipment and vehicles, space and military vehicles, etc.

Toy trucks and animals to sit on or ride.

Dolls for children and collectors: costume dolls and limited signature-editions by Nisbet; "My Little Girl" dolls by Nisbet; Royal Doulton-Nisbet collectors' heirloom dolls.

Teddy bears by Nisbet and others, puppets.

Dolls' dishes and tea sets.

Books: books for children and preteens by Enid Blighton, "Bully Bear" books by Peter Bull, books by Beatrix Potter, "Paddington Bear" books, books of paper dolls in costumes; books that contain paper buildings to assemble, i.e., the "Globe Theater."

Games, puzzles and hobby kits.

Hamleys will be glad to send you specialized manufacturer's catalogs whenever they are available. The toy store itself puts out a general Christmas catalog. All prices are given in pounds sterling. Postage is additional.

Personal checks, international bankers' drafts and credit cards are accepted. An additional 1.6o pounds sterling is charged if you wish to pay by personal check.

The Kite Store
69 Neal Street
Covent Garden
London, WC2H 9PJ
England
Telephone: (011-44-1) 836 1666

Kites of all sizes and descriptions: aerobatic/stunt kites, fighting kites and Chinese kites; kites with geometric shapes: flat, bowed, dihedral, polyhedral, triangular celled kites, square and rhomboid box kites, hexagonal box kites, delta and delta variants and soft kites.

Miscellaneous: hot-air balloon (multicolored mylar), UFO solar balloon (sun-powered), turboprop (rotary-winged kite), Tim Bird (clockwork ornithopter) and the Puddle Jumper (hand-powered flying machine).

Kite-flying accessories: reels, handles, spools, line, tails, windsocks, ground anchors, etc.

Boomerangs and Frisbees.

This is the place for the kite-flying aficionado. There is a brochure describing all of the kites available with the prices given in pounds sterling. There are sixteen brands of kites and each kite is rated as to how easy or difficult it is to assemble and fly.

Postage is additional.

Checks and Visa cards are accepted.

For more toys, *see*

Arabia Rorstrand Center
Cash & Co., Ltd.
Den Permanente A/S
Emerald
Fallers, Ltd.
Harrods
Icemart
Illum
OY Stockmann AB
Rosenthal Studio-Haus
Schweizer Heimatwerk

Alphabetical Index of Sources

Index
of Sources
by Country

About the Authors

ANNE FLATO and MARILYN SCHIFF were both born and raised in Brooklyn and first met while attending Brooklyn College. After graduation they went their separate ways until a few years later when they found that they were neighbors.

They, their husbands and their four children have lived in New Jersey, a few doors apart, for the last seventeen years. Amongst these eight, someone is always traveling abroad, and of course shopping, and bringing back information about great buys and unique products.